This book is dedicated to

LOST AND FOUND

THE TRUE STORY OF THE *STIRLING CASTLE* AND THE DEFAMATION OF DEAL

DAVID CHAMBERLAIN

Copyright David Chamberlain 2008
The moral right of the author has been asserted

All rights reserved. No reproduction, in any form, without prior permission of the author

BEACHES BOOKS
ISBN 978-0-9548439-3-9

CONTENTS

1 INTRODUCTION	5
2 THE BEGINNING OF THE END	8
3 THE GREAT STORM	17
4 THE AFTERMATH	25
5 DEFOE'S DEFAMATION OF DEAL	34
6 LOST AND FOUND	43
7 RECENT SURVEYS	55
8 THE MUSTER LIST	66
9 BIBLIOGRAPHY & ACKNOWLEDGEMENTS	78

INTRODUCTION

The writing of this book has relieved my conscience of two things. Firstly, to justify the vast amount of documentation that I have amassed over the years regarding the *Stirling Castle* and the Great Storm of 1703; and secondly, a chance to put right the wrong that I incurred in my writing of 'The Goodwin Sands Man-of-War'. In that book I insulted the boatmen of Deal by calling them rapacious.

Also, it was the libel of Deal that had perpetuated for over three-hundred years from the pen of one of the biggest rogues of the 17th and 18th century – Daniel Defoe. It is only recently that I have established the truth of what actually happened after that 'dark and stormy night' in 1703.

Optimistically, in this book I have presented these facts to the reader and have dispelled a myth, which in 1705 deeply upset the populace of Deal – so much so that the mayor, Thomas Horne, feared that the townspeople would riot. However, the town corporation's threat of a prosecution for libel and for the story to be rescinded, it appears, was empty.

I offer no excuses for including transcriptions of correspondence from the people who were directly involved with the storm and subsequent events. Again, it must be remembered, that these men wrote about what had happened sometimes only hours after it had occurred. By including this communication it has curbed my somewhat flowery interpretations and, hopefully, not clouded the truth.

I have used my forty years experience as a Deal boatman (now retired) to construe the settings on the beach and in the Downs at that time. The storm of 1703 was comparable to the one of 1987, and again I have used my understanding of what the conditions would have been akin to along the foreshore and out to sea.

By studying the hand written manuscripts of the 1700s it can be seen that often the spelling is put down as it was pronounced. For example, the *Stirling Castle* was nearly always written as Sterling Castle – and occasionally Starling Castle. Therefore names on the muster list do not always completely match with those on the pay list. I have come to a compromise and used those that correspond with similar of today. The eighteenth century penmen, in addition, had a reluctance to use punctuation, which not only makes the sentences long but also difficult to understand. Again I have slightly refined these without distracting from the original.

Another item to be considered is that the early dates that I have used are from the Julius calendar and to render these to 'now' time (Gregorian calendar), one should add eleven days.

Through research I have come to the conclusion that navy life in the early part of the eighteenth century was not quite as harsh as it would be a hundred years later. Experienced seamen had fulfilment in their calling and most were educated enough to have the ability to read and write. Although their wages were seldom paid on time, they still had the security of being fed, receive hospital treatment and get a pension or compensation if they became wounded in action.

Even though I had previous knowledge of the *Stirling Castle* shipwreck, my own personal involvement did not materialise until I was invited to join *Seadive* as a professional boatman in 1999. It was in that year when the protected wreck site licensee, Bob Peacock, decided that a detailed underwater survey of the *Stirling Castle* was required. His organisation *Seadive* (acronym for South East Archaeological Divers) prearranged that an in-depth assessment of the wreck – which was re-emerging from the sand wave – should be undertaken. This expedition was aptly named 'Operation Man-of-War' and, when it was undertaken, a vast amount of data was recorded.

The ultimate fate of the *Stirling Castle* is unclear. As the sand withdraws from acting as a cradle, the wreck has started to collapse and untold artefacts are being destroyed. It must be appreciated, that the previous appraisals have been undertaken by amateur archaeological divers – at their own expense. Furthermore, it should be a priority that the government increase funding for our underwater heritage; that is being lost and forgotten by those politicians with an 'out of sight, out of mind' mentality.

There seems to be a mistrust amongst the enthusiastic, amateur archaeological diver and the paid professional. The amateur feels restricted with rules and regulations and the professional suspect conspiracy, with accusations bordering on treasure hunting – similar to the land based archaeologist and the metal detectorist.

Perhaps there never will be a perfect balance between the draconian government policies and the amateur diving archaeologists – especially in times when more and more legislation and restrictions are being considered. This unfortunate fact will only further annoy the diver and underwater explorer, to a point where they will become secretive and keep what ever they find to themselves – and ultimately deny the nation of its rightful heritage. With forethought, perhaps a strategy could be found, that in theory can be standardised, however could also be adapted to the conditions for each individual wreck site.

If this book has been of interest to the reader, then I recommend a visit to the Thanet Maritime Museum, situated in the Clock House on the quayside at Ramsgate Harbour. Run by the East Kent Maritime Trust, the museum houses a vast amount of artefacts that have been discovered and conserved from the *Stirling Castle*. Their most recent item being the magnificent 'Rupertinoe' 32 pounder cannon and carriage.

David Chamberlain 2008

The author aboard the dive boat *Tusker II*

THE BEGINNING OF THE END

At the cessation of the Third Dutch War in 1674, Samuel Pepys, MP and Secretary of the Admiralty, realised that the Royal Navy was old and battered. He knew that our nearest and traditional enemies, the Dutch and French, were building a larger fleet of ships than Britain could cope with. If, and when the nation went to war again the security of Britain's dominance of the sea would have been put in jeopardy. They would not only have been outnumbered in battle — but also would have lost the financial lifeline of trade with the rest of the world.

His pleas with Parliament and King Charles II, in 1675, were reluctantly heard and passed with a shipbuilding programme of 30 great ships to be completed over the following two years. Of these ships, there would be one first rate, nine second rates and twenty third rates that were to be built in the dockyards. The vast sum of £600,000 was put aside from the near bankrupt government for the expense.

It was estimated that at least three thousand trees would be needed to build a third rate ship; therefore it did not take long before the much prized seasoned grown timber was used up and trees were then hastily cut from the royal parks. When they became scarce, wood subsequently had to be shipped in by sea as it was too difficult to transport the large logs by road.

The keel of the *Stirling Castle* was laid down in the Royal Dockyard at Deptford in 1677. John Shish was the master shipwright who would oversee the warship to her last coat of Stockholm tar and red paint on the rampant lion figurehead. Shish and his team of carpenters made the ship ready for her launch on 28th July, 1679.

The *Stirling Castle* was classed as a third rate vessel of 151 feet 2 inches with a beam of 40 feet 4 inches. Her top and main gun decks carried a total of 70 cannon, comprising of the largest at 32-pounders to three-pounders mounted on her poop deck. These third rate vessels were to be likened to the modern day frigate or even the destroyer. They had more manoeuvrability than the cumbersome first and second rates of 84 to 100 guns, yet they still had enough fire power to inflict considerable damage; and would be the mainstay of the Royal Navy for many years.

King Charles II attended *Stirling Castle's* topping-out ceremony, which was a lavish affair of food and drink, to celebrate the completion and work done by the carpenters and labourers. The cost of this party became so expensive that the Admiralty advised Shish not to participate in another one in the future without their consent.

Possibly, the new fleet of warships acted as a deterrent, as it would not be until 1690 that the French were again at war with the British. During the peace, the majority of the fleet had been laid up at Chatham, and when they were being made ready for sea, it was found that parts of their timbers had become rotten. This malady was due either to lack of maintenance, the fresh water of the River Medway or even the green unseasoned timber used in part of their construction.

Nevertheless, the *Stirling Castle*, along with the rest of the fleet, went to sea and fought in the battle of Beachy Head and was present at the victorious battle of Barfleur in 1692. This action ensured that the French would no longer venture out from their ports. The *Stirling Castle* spent the rest of the war escorting merchant ships, until the cessation of conflict in 1697.

Two years later it was necessary to rebuild the *Stirling Castle* in the dockyard of Chatham; where all of her loose and decayed timbers were replaced. With the threat of another war with France, she was starting to be made ready in March, 1701. Following her stores, guns and everything else (which included a new bell) being placed aboard, her masts were raised into place and her newly refurbished rigging tightened.

With the completion of her refit, she proceeded to the Downs and then to Spithead, where Captain John Johnson took over command from her temporary captain. This was to be Johnson's first term of duty since peace had been last made with France, four years previous.

The *Stirling Castle* spent the rest of that year on escort duty and eventually in January 1702 she was berthed at Plymouth where the vessel was dry-docked and careened. After a general overhaul she went back to her sea duties and with the death of King William III and the accession to the throne of Queen Anne this would be the fourth monarch that the ship was to serve under.

On May 4th Britain declared war on France and Spain. At the time of the announcement *Stirling Castle* was on an assignment to bring back four companies of troops from Ireland. When they were disembarked at Spithead the vessel stayed moored up until mid June. Then, along with a squadron of 28 ships, she was dispatched to Cape Finisterre to await the main fleet under the command of Sir George Rooke. However, the admiral's aim of taking Cadiz was thwarted, and by late September the vessels were ordered back to England.

When the *Stirling Castle*, *Eagle*, *Pembroke* and five horse transport ships put into Lagos Bay to replenish their empty water casks; it was there that they gained intelligence of a Spanish treasure fleet – being escorted by 30 French warships – that were at Virgo Bay. This news was promptly relayed to the main fleet and an attack on Redondela Harbour was brought in-force. Soldiers were landed to take out the fort and gun batteries and the warship *Association* bombarded and destroyed another battery of 20 guns near by. With the harbour's defences being dealt with, the 80-gun *Torbay* smashed through the harbour's boom barricade and a ferocious sea battle then erupted with the Anglo-Dutch fleet against the French and Spanish. The outcome was that the Allied ships won a glorious victory, restored naval reputation and enhanced the near empty coffers of the treasury with some Spanish silver.

Meanwhile, the *Stirling Castle* was battering against heavy seas on her way back to England. On 8th October, the rough weather was enough to strain the planks of the ship and four feet of water was found in the bilge. It took four hours of continuous pumping to clear it. Then, the mizzen mast split in two and the main mast became unstable. Curling waves crashed aboard the *Stirling Castle's* deck smashing the ship's yawl, creating chaos amid the struggling seamen. They briefly put in at Dartmouth and subsequently docked at Portsmouth for repairs.

Whilst the man-of-war was moored in Portsmouth Harbour, Vice-Admiral John Leake and his entourage went aboard on the 23rd of December. Although a son of a navy gunner, he eventually became Admiral Sir John Leake; and it was partly due to his efforts, in 1707, that England took the much needed Mediterranean base at Port Mahon, Minorca. This was to become the necessary harbour that the allied fleet needed in the Mediterranean.

For him, the ship's hospitality included Christmas and the first three weeks of January, 1703. In the appropriate column, the muster list acknowledged his departure with dfs (discharged from ship). At the same time as John Leake was aboard the *Stirling Castle*, the ship moved to Spithead and on the 13th January 1703 she started taking on sea provisions.

Five days later, according to the muster list, 125 marines of Colonel Saunderson's Regiment started to arrive; although the completion of the company, under Captain David Ward and Captain Abington, was not totally concluded until the beginning of July that year. Saunderson's marines were formed in 1702, and they were a re-formation of Saunderson's regiment of foot, originally raised in 1689. This regiment fought in the Low Countries during King William's war against Louis XIV of France. They had earned particular distinction at the storming of the great fortress of Namur, in 1695, and were disbanded at the end of hostilities in 1698.

The following month orders were received that *Stirling Castle* would be part of a squadron of other third rate vessels that were to escort 120 merchant ships to Portugal. She left the confines of British waters on 11th February and found sea conditions rough with gale force winds. Within four days, the crew's discomforts were further burdened with short allowance of all victuals aboard the ship. Although the men would receive a small increase in their wages, this was no consolation to the hardships, and an empty stomach, when weathering the Bay of Biscay in a storm.

Before the vessel reached the anchorage at Lisbon two marines died, and whilst she was there a further seven soldiers expired. The cause was an apparent lack of food and drink and three marine privates mutinied over their deprivation. At their court martial on March 21st the record of the findings state:

> *That Uriah Williams be shot to death at the head of the companies of the regiment at Canterbury within 20 days and not before 14 from the date of the President's signature to the proceedings of the court.*

The sentence for the other two was slightly less harsh:

> *That John Bolton do run the gauntlet 4, several times through such part of the regiment as the Commanding Officer may direct, and that Francis Griffen do run the gauntlet three.*

By the end of March, *Stirling Castle* was away from Lisbon and moving up the coast. However, further orders on the 7th April had her detached from the other men-of-war for the purpose of escorting ten merchantmen from the estuary and port of Viana – to join the main fleet for their journey home. The weather was adverse, and they battled against a head wind.

Before they made the Isle of Scilly lighthouse on 14th May another three marines were logged in the muster as DD (Discharged Dead). It took a few more days for the ships to enter into the Plymouth Sound and on the 18th the vessel was re-supplied with stores and the crew were on whole allowance once more.

Even though the time limit had passed for the sentence on the mutinous marines, it seems that an application for clemency was applied to Queen Anne. She graciously gave a pardon to Uriah Williams and remited the punishment ordered on the other two. Apparently it was revealed that the marines had embarked on to the *Stirling Castle*: ' *...before being paid by the Victualling Department the sums due for the savings on ship's rations during the former cruise.*' Queen Anne's husband, Prince George of Denmark, who was also Lord High Admiral: '*...expressed his serious displeasure with the Department and ordered a victualling officer to go at once to the quarters of the marine company, wherever they might be, and to pay the men.*' The Paymaster for Colonel Sanderson's regiment, it seems, was reluctant to part with the money.

The stigma of non payment of dues to the soldiers followed them until their disbandment from their Canterbury barracks, in 1714. This time it would be Sergeants John Martin and Steven Pearce, both whom had served on the *Stirling Castle*, who revolted against the hierarchy for remittance of their full pay. However, instead of clemency, they were arrested and charged before a civil magistrate with riot and misdemeanour.

In the month of May, 1703, England completed the 'Methuen Treaties' with Portugal. It seemed that this pact was more to do with developing the export trade than to be political, and it encouraged the English to participate in port wine instead of French claret. It is not known which was preferred, however, there accrued an increase in the ailment of gout throughout the English male population. Nevertheless, it gave the allied fleet important forward base harbours in the Atlantic and a gateway to the Mediterranean, until the taking of Minorca in 1707.

With the *Stirling Castle* still in Plymouth and a summer campaign not yet underway, some of the crew became restless. It was known that they would be sailing in the near future – yet, the men noticed that victuals were not being loaded aboard. From May until the 2nd of July a total of twenty-two much needed seamen (mainly AB's) jumped ship. Along with them, fourteen marines did likewise; forgoing any pay owed to them.

It was recorded on the 2nd of July that the ship: *'Began short allowance of all species, beer excepted'.*

The *Stirling Castle* sailed soon after, to join the fleet under the command of Sir Cloudsley Shovell. When they met up at Lands End, Captain Johnson received orders that his vessel, along with the third rate ship of the line *Swiftsure*, were to escort merchantmen into the Portuguese harbours of Porto and Viana. By the last week of July both men-of-war were again reunited with the rest of the squadron.

Unfortunately, this summer offensive into the Mediterranean faired miserably. Starting late, low on supplies and with too few of their Dutch allies, very little was achieved. The larger first and second rate ships suffered more casualties, not from battle, but of lack of food and sickness. A decision was made to return to England and winter in home waters.

Shortly before the orders were confirmed to re-join Sir Cloudsley Shovell's fleet, *Stirling Castle* continued her routine escort duties. On receiving the orders, and on the homeward journey, it was logged that a quick stop at Altea, on the 17th September, two marines managed to '*run*' (desert) from the ship.

A short allowance of wine ten days later possibly caused some inconvenience to *Stirling Castle's* officers. Nonetheless, it was a credit to John Hollows, the purser aboard the warship, that there was very little mortality through lack of food amongst the seamen; although some had to be transferred to the *Sara* and *Betty* hospital ships.

It was recorded that the vessel began whole allowance of all provisions, beer excepted, on 29th October and on 8th November they had the luxury of drinking fresh water. Apparently the provisions had been sent by sea, in desperation of their severe situation. Sadly the rest of the fleet had endured 1500 deaths and had filled the three hospital ships to capacity.

Winter was beginning to take a bite when Shovell's squadron reached the Isle of Wight on the 16th November and entered the Downs, off Deal, the following day. It would be on that day that Robert Drew, the master's mate, Pollycarqus Taylor, a midshipman, two captains servants, one AB (Able Bodied seaman) and two ordinary seamen left *Stirling Castle* and were '*Lent a merchant shippe*'. Which merchant vessel or why they were lent is not acknowledged. It is also not known if these men returned aboard, as there is no record of it in the muster, however, only two survived to be paid on the 2nd May 1704.

Three days later on the 20th November, Sir Cloudsley gave the order that the *Assistance* and *Stirling Castle* should return down Channel and escort *Nassau*, another third rate, back to the Downs. This ship had unfortunately grounded on an uncharted bank off Beachy Head and badly damaged her rudder. When the *Nassau* was found, it was left to the *Stirling Castle* to secure a tow. On the way back to the Downs, at 2 o'clock that afternoon, they passed a Dutch Vice Admiral in his warship that did not salute or lower his flag. This was deemed as a courtesy in English waters and Captain John Johnson commanded that a round should be fired from one of the *Stirling Castle's* cannon. The Dutch vessel immediately conformed to the request. This was the last time that the *Stirling Castle* would fire her ordnance in anger.

Arriving back in the Downs on the 22nd, they found the weather fresh, with strong south-west winds. As they settled at anchor, the muster-master James Beverly came aboard. He totalled up the check and eventually left with the last and only surviving document from aboard the *Stirling Castle* – the muster book. Furthermore, on that same day, the entire company of marines left the ship and were ferried onto the third rate, *Royal Oak* – this fortunate move helped save their lives, as this ship would weather the incoming storm.

Admiral Sir Cloudsley Shovell realised that the Downs was not an area to linger in, with his massive bluff sided first and second rate ships. Although the Downs was a perfect anchorage in normal circumstances he knew that if a ship dragged or lost an anchor with the arriving spring tides and wind, it would become a critical situation. Over two hundred ships lay riding at anchor in close formation and the Goodwin Sands were located a mere two or three miles to the east.

The Goodwin Sands in more benign weather

On 24th November, the wind and sea conditions had not moderated and the Admiral ordered his large warships and hospital ships to accompany him and set sail for the River Medway. Chatham, it was thought, would have been the ideal place to winter his vessels. He left the smaller third, fourth and fifth rates in the capable hands of Rear-Admiral Beaumont, commander of the Channel Fleet.

Sir Basil Beaumont, it seems, was an up and coming sailor with a great career ahead of him. Born in 1669 he became the fifth son of Sir Henry Beaumont. His childhood in Leicestershire could not have been lonely as his father managed to sire a total of twenty-one brothers and sisters. Basil had gone to sea at an early age and had made lieutenant at eighteen and given his first command before he reached twenty-one years old. Now he was Rear-Admiral of the Blue and in command of the Channel Squadron and he knew the waters that surrounded the Downs well. Curiously, he had made his berth and flagship on the *Mary*, a fourth rate ship of more than fifty years old; although she was a vessel that had served with distinction throughout that time.

The only large ship that was now left in the Downs was the *Prince George*, a second rate of 80 guns. Onboard were Vice Admiral Leake and his captain, Steven Martin. They had suffered great hardships, due to the Admiralties lack of supplying sufficient victuals throughout the campaign in the Mediterranean. There had been a loss of sixty mariners aboard the *Prince George*, and the rest of the ships' company were in poor physical shape. Little did they know that they had the worse to come?

The fury of the storm erupts

THE 'GREAT STORM'

Hurricanes do not occur in Britain, however, winds that surpass hurricane force on the Beaufort scale do. Admiral Sir Francis Beaufort created the scale in 1805 to help sailors estimate the strength of winds by their visual observations. Two years later he made a slight amendment which created the maximum wind force of 12 or hurricane force. When the winds reached and exceeded the strength of 73 mph (miles per hour) the sailor would view: *'huge waves; air filled with foam; sea completely white with driving spray; visibility greatly reduced'*.

The wind speed of the 'Great Storm', on Saturday, 27th November 1703, probably reached gusts of 150 mph. This storm could be arguably the worst England had ever witnessed as it caused the destruction of property and death of more people than any before or since.

The weather that preceded the 'Great Storm' was adverse enough to be noted as exceptional, with successions of Atlantic depressions sweeping over southern England. Warships in the Downs were reluctantly lowering and raising their yards and topmasts as the gales came and went. This chore would lessen the windage on the anchored vessels. Because the anchorage in the Downs was close to the Goodwin Sands, the ships' captains knew this tiresome labour was necessary. However, they recognised that if a ship needed to manoeuvre in an emergency then she would need the benefit of her sails.

On the day that Admiral Shovell decided to move part of his fleet of large three-deck ships to the north, the routine of shipboard life in the other vessels carried on regardless. The captain's log on the third rate *Shrewsbury* stated that:

> *24th November, 1703.*
> *Hazy weather and very fresh gales. About nine last night struck yards and topmasts and at daylight this morning got them up again. This morning Sir Cloudsley Shovell sailed hence in the* Triumph *for Chatham, taking with him Sir Stafford Fairborn, Vice Admiral of the Red in the* Association, *with* St George, Royal Oak, Revenge,

Cambridge *and* Russell *also some other fire-ships, hospital-ships etc. This afternoon took in, out of a Dover Hoy, 13 butts of beer 7 firkins of butter and 30 cheeses, and put out with empty casks that the Hoy could carry.*

The next two days leading up to the tempest, the master made the following entry into the *Prince George's* log:

25th November, 1703.
Moderate gales; fair weather the latter part; strong gales showery weather.

26th November, 1703.
Strong gales, with thick and showery weather. At eight last night, we veered out the long service which is two cables and a half. Shortened in the small bower cables, put service on him.

Not only was the lengthening of the second rate *Prince George's* anchor cables a governing factor of her survival, but also that they had been renewed before she had left port for the Mediterranean. Many of the other vessels let out more anchor cable, however, old and rotten rope would not protect them from the severity of the wind and tide that they would encounter in the following 24 hours.

On the night of the 26th a deep and desperate low pressure formed over an area close to Liverpool. Those few people who had a barometer watched the mercury fall to a record low. Daniel Defoe wrote that he: '*...accused my children of breaking the instrument when I could not see the quicksilver in its glass bowl.*'

The beginning of the storm started off in the West Country just before midnight and hit with a fury that many would remember for the rest of their lives. Bristol bore an enormous amount of constructional and financial damage – as the tiles were lifted off the merchants and shipowners warehouses and the cellars, full of tobacco and perishable goods, were flooded by the surge of the River Severn bursting its banks. The south-west wind swept through the counties of Somerset, Hampshire, Sussex and then into Kent.

The ships in the Downs were starting to strain at their anchors, feeling the pressure of the increasing wind as it rose to a severe gale. High tide just after midnight and a new moon meant that the flow of water would be strong on the spring flood tide. Along with a high spring tide through this part of the Channel it could be expected that the run of water would reach two or three knots. However, with this extraordinary increase of wind blowing the same direction as the tide then it would be fair to speculate that the current would run at a speed of up to six knots and more.

Concern for the ships' safety was indicated by many of the captains as they entered in their logs that about two o'clock in the morning the wind had increased to a violent storm. In desperation some of the vessels lowered a sheet anchor to help reduce the drag and prevent driving on to the other ships. Even with both bowers and the sheet anchor streaming out ahead, ships still dragged in the congested haven.

By three o'clock the wind had increased to a fury that none of them had ever witnessed before. In the next hour, apprehension was felt by the officers and crew aboard all of the vessels that were weathering the raging storm.

As it was a new moon, the shipboard men had to work in pitch-black surroundings – although there was white spume all around them. In the midst of mountainous seas breaking over the ships' bows – sounding like the report of cannon – it was not possible to keep the lanterns alight with the force of wind and spray. The reverberation of wind screaming through the miles of rigging made any form of giving orders nigh impossible. At the height of the storm it would have been difficult to have faced the wind and breathe, and with the rolling motion of the ship, hard to stand. It is not feasible to comprehend the terror and confusion that these soaking-wet, cold men – already weakened from three months of short allowance and sickness – must have endured.

With the raging wind and tide, some of the ships started to drag their anchors. The *Prince George's* captain was thankful of his new anchors and cables as the hundred and fifty feet *Restoration* dragged her anchor on to the second rate's best bower anchor. They lay together for half an hour until the *Restoration's* cable parted and she driven away with the storm. The following day, when the

Prince George hove in her anchors they could see where the other warship's gear had rubbed on their cable.

While all this was going on in the Downs, the adjacent town of Deal was also getting a battering. The navy-yard store man, and future mayor of Deal, Thomas Warren penned:

> ... it has blown down all the east and west fence walls of the buildings that are erected here for Her Majesties service and blown a great part of the piling of the great storehouse, boat houses and dwelling houses. It has blown down the gibbet of the pirate that hung in chains at the south end of the town and washed the man to sea. It has likewise blown down all the grain mills herewith, beat down some houses and un-tiled and damaged most of the others in town.

Out at sea more dramas were unfolding and the captain of the *Dunwich* wrote in his log:

> The gale increasing at 3 this morning it blew a most violent storm and our anchors coming home (dragging) we drove within a quarter cable's length of the *Nassau* and fearing of driving through his hawse, which we could no way avoid and we cut our fore-main and mizzen mast by the board. Then brought up and rid fast. One man killed and 2 wounded with the fall of the fore mast.

Lord Archibald Hamilton on the *Eagle* noted that:

> We heard several guns fired by ships in distress and some drove by us on both sides, between 4 and 5 o'clock the Gaurland *drove on board us upon the starboard bow, we veered away on both anchors to get clear but being entangled he lay upon our bow till all his masts came by the board, then drove along side and brought up astern of us, we by great providence stood fast, our mainsail by his yards was tore loose as far as the clewgarnet block and beat with much violence, there was no possibility of*

> *stowing it, our spritsail blowing lose we cut the yard as also the spritsail topmast by the board, all this while his masts and rigging were lying thwart our hawse it was 9 this morning before we could cut them clear, our longboat was sunk by the storm in the night; at daylight, not being able to strike our top gallant masts, we cut them away and got our top yards down.*

Although the third rate warship *Eagle* recorded that guns were being fired in distress, there was no chance of help. Therefore, perhaps, they were being fired as a warning to other vessels that *they* were dragging anchor and to keep clear, or sheer away if possible.

Meanwhile, the *Stirling Castle* was also having problems with her own anchors driving through the ground. She managed to lose her best and second best bower, however, the ship held when a third anchor got a hold in a patch of clay. The cause for the loss of these essential anchors could possibly have occurred when, according to Thomas Warren after talking to survivors of the *Stirling Castle* two days later, wrote that:

> ... *those people that are brought ashore can give no certain accord of the* Northumberland *and* Restoration, *some say the former drove foul of their ship,* Stirling Castle, *and put them away...*

By the time the tide had eased, there was no indication that the wind would abate as well. It seemed to get worse and when the ebb tide made an effort to run against the direction of the wind, the frictions heightened the waves. Around about five in the morning, those ships still at anchor rolled mercilessly in the beam-on mountainous seas. The ebb was not strong enough, against the wind, to swing them around and receive the massive waves on their counters.

This dilemma would have affected the entirety of those stricken vessels. Masts, that had survived, were cut by the board (removed to deck level) to help alleviate the roll. Floating debris would have become a hazard to the other vessels and damage on or below the waterline must have occurred.

Fortunately for the *Stirling Castle*, the area where she lay was in the shoal water of the Bunt Head – an outcrop of the Goodwin Sands. It was here that a curious phenomenon of the Sands happens. In the shoal water of 10 to 3 fathoms (60 to 18 feet) the tide on the west side of the main Goodwins bank tends to take a different path to the norm. In this shoal water it is often calmer, and the tide, sometimes known as the 'young flood', runs to the north hours before it would either side of the bank. This occurrence of comparative calmness only happens in a south-westerly blow where wind and tide run in the same direction. On tranquil days, with light south-west winds, the 'young flood' can actually be heard approaching, and can be seen rushing and flowing in the shoal water, often creating small whirlpools.

Stirling Castle starts to founder

It can only be speculated at the cause of the *Stirling Castle's* demise. A cannon could have broken loose in the violent rolling and stove out a lower gun port. With the inflow of sea, through the open port, it would have been difficult to keep the water level from rising in the bilge. Perhaps a floating mast struck and sprung some of her planks, again letting the sea enter the ship. Fatigue and hypothermia would claim the crew and a back breaking turn at the chain pumps would have left them listless and gasping for breath. However, necessitate for survival often gives added strength – and these men would have a long wait to contemplate on their endurance.

What is known, is that the *Stirling Castle* sank at anchor and was not dashed to pieces on the Goodwin Sands. The surviving anchor that held her was discovered by diving marine archaeologists in August 2002. They confirmed that it was complete with stock and was of the same size as the vessel would have carried – also it was found nearly one cable (160 m) away from the bow alignment of the shipwreck. The other two anchors of 42 and 45 hundredweight (2138.2 kg and 2290.9 kg), that the Stirling Castle lost, were found by the Deal boatmen shortly after the storm. The Admiralty reclaimed and identified these by the name of the vessel carved into their stocks and on the nunn buoys attached to their rings.

Another clue that the Goodwins bank had not claimed her was that the rudder – always the first item to be lost in a violent grounding – was still in situ when she was discovered by divers in 1979.

Whatever the cause, by daylight, there was enough of her stern-castle above the sea for the men's temporary deliverance. The vessel's keel had settled on to the gently sloping shoal bank, on which either side the seas broke with malice. With their ship aground all they could do was wait and pray for salvation.

It is known that the survival of many ships was due to, either holding at anchor; or setting a little sail and successfully attempting to sail through the Gull Stream and away from the Goodwins; or, owing to a shallow draft, were swept over the Sands at high tide and into deeper water on the other side. The unlucky ones, with the lack of sea room, would have dragged into each other and unable to get free, pounded themselves to pieces. Other vessels would have been overwhelmed by the sheer force of the sea that cascaded and crashed upon their decks. Those that hit the Goodwin Sands rapidly broke into matchwood, as the surf beat them to almost a pulp.

For those mariners in the Downs that survived England's most terrible storm it could be summed up in the words from the captain of the *Shrewsbury*: '...*and through God's mercy our ship rid fast.*'

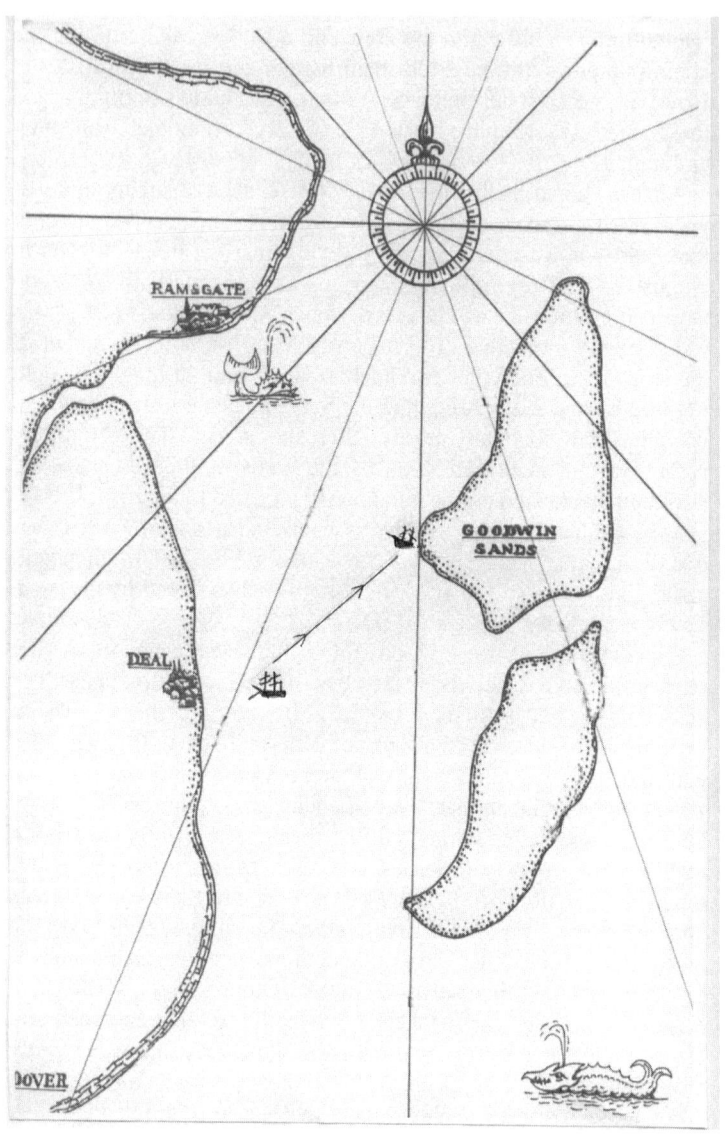

The direction that the Stirling Castle dragged her anchor into the shoal water of the Bunt Head. Her final resting place 51°16'.46"N. 01°30'.41"E.

THE AFTERMATH

As dawn broke, the aftermath of the storm – which was still blowing strong – could be encountered. Thomas Warren wrote to the Admiralty:

> *Deal the 27th November 1703*
> *I am sorry I must account Your Honour of a miserable slaughter that has happened amongst shipping in the Downs. Yesterday it blew very hard all day, but about midnight it came on so violent at SW (South West) and continued between that and the WSW (West South West) that about two in the morning several guns were to be fired from ships in distress, but there being such a hurricane it was impossible for a man to stand against it, so much more to afford them any help from the shore that out of about 100 sail of one sort or another there is not above 70 now to be seen, and a great many of them floating only bottoms, having I presume cut their mast by the board the better to ride it out.*

On board the *Prince George*, the men marvelled that their high sided warship had not been blown away. In a later publication about their captain it said of the 'miracle':

> *Captain Martin, considering the time of year, and foreseeing the storm, had taken all the means to secure the ship that human prudence could suggest, which under Providence, was the preservation of his own and the lives in the ship. He had made a snug ship, and veered out three long service to two cables and two-thirds, which enabled him not only to ride out the storm himself, but to do what was hardly ever known upon a like occasion, which was to ride another ship, and that of a seventy-gun ship too.*

Although the ill-fated third rate *Restoration* was only secured to the *Prince George's* anchors for half an hour, it must have felt like a lifetime to the seamen. Those who survived the 'Great Storm' would, no doubt, have stories similar to this to enthral, and eventually bore, those who would be willing to listen.

As the storm started to abate, the ships' captains and officers took stock of the situation. The sea would have been littered with wood, masts and tangled cordage – amongst it, also, the bodies of the lost sailors. To the north-east of Deal, the hulls of shipwrecks could be observed and, with the aid of a spyglass, men were seen clinging to the upper decks and masts that showed above the waves. Thomas Warren's account, written on that same day, can describe the devastation at sea better than any contemporary author:

> *Of the men-of-war, Rear Admiral Beaumont in the* Mary *is missing, with the* Northumberland, Restoration, Stirling Castle *and* Mortar Bomb. *The* Prince George, Essex, Assistance, Shrewsbury, Eagle, Content, Chatham, Mary Galley *and* Hunter Fire-ship *rid it out with all their masts, but the* Nassau *has cut away her main mast; the* Guarland *and* Dunwich *all their masts, and the* Postillion Prize *her main mast and mizzen mast, and there are five great ships and two small ones that ride to the northward with all their masts by the board, two of them we take to be men-of-war. It's a miserable spectacle to behold the ships in the Downs as they now ride torn almost to pieces by this storm, and the like weather has not been known in the memory of any man here, for when the ship broke away, as the greatest part of them did about five in the morning, most flashes of gun being then seen, and the wind being then highest at WSW; they could not carry a knot of sail to hug the shore; that is feared the Goodwin Sand broke up most of them, for when it was light we could see five sail, two of them pretty big ships fast upon it, one I am afraid was a man-of-war by the number of men we could discern to shelter themselves upon the masts, who all perished as the water flowed and the sea broke upon her, and there is little of them now to be seen. There are likewise three small vessels sunk in the road.*

At first light the Deal boatmen would have emerged from their dwellings. Not many could have slept through that night with the frenzy of the storm raging outside. Some would have spent the time in the darkness seeing to their boats. Their craft would have been beached close to the houses that lined the foreshore. These abodes had given a lee from the offshore wind, but not from the flying roof tiles. The longshoremen would have busied themselves using extra chocks and lashing, which made the small boats fast and secure to their capstans.

Nonetheless, the surf would be still crashing ashore on the beach – with the largest waves occurring at the noonday high-water, leaving a dangerous swell and drawback as the tide receded. No boats could get afloat, as it would take the longshoremen a day with their shovels to make the beach suitable for a launch.

Meanwhile, aboard the ships in the Downs, the raffle of cordage that lay about the vessels' decks would have had to be stowed, replaced or spliced. Carpenters and their crews prepared lists of items that had been broken or destroyed, and lieutenants noted which masts, yards and spars needed replacing. The majority of their yawls and longboats, some which had been left moored to the mother ship, were either sunk or damaged beyond repair. Many of the captains realised that they would have to wait for a hoy or a hooker to come out to them; to receive their requests for replacement equipment and materials.

Those ships that were still in danger of collision from the near proximity of their neighbours must have hove up their anchors and found a safer place to settle. The urgency of the situation would have been the only reason for this action, as the damage that had been done to their ships made it barely possible for the captains to con their vessels.

When the tide rose, the wrecks that were visible on the horizon started to disappear. Vice-Admiral Leake, made a signal for all surviving ships' boats to be lowered and make ready to save lives. Once these small craft were away from the lee of the shore the sea conditions worsened; and with darkness engulfing the short afternoon the boats were recalled without any results. Sailors on board a yawl made a gallant attempt to rescue lives from a wreck before the recall – and failed. After they reported to the Vice

Admiral aboard the *Prince George,* the master wrote in his log: *The boat came and said they saw men onboard her* (the wreck) *but could not possibly get to her, the sea so great.*

John Leake was saddened and frustrated by the loss of life that occurred that day. It had been in less than 24 hours that over a thousand men had perished in the anchorage of the Downs.

The following day, the storm had subsided; nevertheless it was still blowing hard from the south-west. Almost in irony a captain wrote: ... *moderate weather to which hath been of late, yet still very fresh gales.*

On that day, Thomas Warren had arisen early. After the storm his tireless work for the Admiralty was never ending. His investigation into the naval storehouse showed that he had barely one anchor cable that was only suitable for a fourth rate ship. He put pen to paper and requested that the Navy Board send a couple of vessels with spare masts, rigging and stores.

The trusted local boatmen that were employed by the Admiralty would have had their boats ready for a launch through the surf as they awaited orders from Warren. To oversee that every possible relief for the ships could be administered, the Admiralty store keeper even went afloat himself. He later wrote to the Navy Board:

> *Deal 28th November 1703.*
> *Since mine to your Honour of yesterday by express, the weather has been much that I have been afloat and those ships that ride to the nor-ward without masts prove to be the* Antelope *hospital ship, a great Hamburger and three English merchantmen. That the* Restoration, Stirling Castle, Northumberland, Mary *and* Mortar Bomb *are still missing and the four former said certain to be lost upon the Goodwin Sand and if so all men lost, tho there is a hull of one of them to be seen, that I have sent boats to see what men can be saved, there being a waft seen from her at daylight, which are not yet come ashore...*

It had been a busy day for Warren and he had tried to visit as many warships as he could under those conditions. His list of equipment needed from some of the captains grew. The store keeper's diligence can be assessed by the conclusion of his letter to the Board:

> ...*The* Warspright *and* Litchfield *came into the Downs the Friday afternoon before the storm and held it out, the latter with the loss of her foremast. About noon the* Torbay *came into the Downs from the westward without a fore topmast. I find here will to be great want of cordage, jury masts, anchors and cables to service those ships that are left; that I do enclose your Honours account of what I have by me that you may please the better to order a fitting supply to answer their demands; tho I cannot yet have a particular account from the commander of what is wanting, but the* Prince George *and some others want cables as I presume Vice Admiral Leake has given an account of this day by express. The* Antelope *Hospital wants an anchor and cable to secure her and likewise jury mast which the captain has signified to the Vice-Admiral and desired his assistance, but he has sent his treatise to me, and it is not in my power to help him.*
> *I am with respect. TW*

When the craft that Warren had dispatched came upon the only wreck that was seen showing a waft (signal of distress), it turned out to be the *Stirling Castle*. The survivors were barely alive as they held on to anything that their frozen fingers could clutch. By this time, the hull of the ship had almost disappeared and what clothing remained on the sailors was soaked and in shreds. Most of the men were hypothermic and in a state of delirium. All around them they had witnessed the other wrecks breaking up and disappearing under the waves as the tide made. They had seen men perish and knew it would only be a matter of time before they would succumb to the same fate. What would have been their joy when they saw the small beach boats coming to their rescue?

The half dead sailors were plucked off the waterlogged hulk with haste. The phenomenon of that slightly calmer shoal water on the edge of the Bunt Head was their salvation.

With the hours of daylight scarce, the Deal boatmen would have made their way back to the shore, by either rowing or sailing as close to the wind as they could. Once ashore, the men were offloaded and given clothing for their freezing bodies and food for their nourishment.

Weariness from his day afloat did not stop Thomas Warren from arising early the following day. He read his dispatches from the Admiralty, and was informed of what had occurred with the survivors and wrote out another report for the Board:

> *Deal the 29th November 1703*
>
> *I have received your Honours of yesterday by express and shall acquaint commanders of Her Majesties ships in the Downs, that you have been pleased to give orders for the hastening to them supplies of anchors, cables, cordage and other stores, and in the mean time nothing shall be wanting in me that can be done here towards their relief.*
>
> *The wreck I gave your Honour an account in mine of yesterday that was seen to have a waft out at the Goodwin Sand, proved to be the* Stirling Castle *the boats that went from hence, and one that went from Ramsgate having saved about 70 of her men, in such number is four officers of the marines, the third lieutenant, the Chaplain and cook of the ship, the rest of the officers and men being drowned. Amongst this number that was saved belonging to the* Stirling Castle *was one of the* Mary's *company who was coxswain of her yawl; he gives an account that she parted with all her cables and drove upon the Goodwin where she soon broke to pieces,. He saw Rear Admiral Beaumont upon a piece of her quarter with his clerk and Lieutenant Sampson; and this man got upon another piece of wreck, and by swimming from one piece to another he was drove to the* Stirling Castle *with two men more, who died as soon as they got aboard; that this man is all that is saved of the* Mary's *company, those people that are brought ashore can give no certain accord of the* Northumberland *and* Restoration, *some say the former drove foul of their ship* Stirling Castle *and put them away, and soon after she sank down, and others that*

> *they were both lost upon the sands, but I am afraid tis too certain that they are gone, and none of their company's saved to give any account of them; The* Mortar Bomb *is also still missing, and no manner of account to be had of her. As soon as I can get the particulars of what is wanting to each ship, shall send it to your Honour with an account of what occurs.*
> *Being with respect   TW*

Thomas Atkins, coxswain of the flagship *Mary's* yawl, must have been the luckiest man to have endured the storm. The chances of being the sole survivor from his ship, and ending up on the deck of the only wreck left intact in the Downs, is almost unbelievable. The captain of the *Mary*, Edward Hopson, was also most fortunate as he was ashore on business at the time of his ship's loss. At his court-martial (a naval requirement for any captain who loses his ship) it was written: *… that he had to go to London on some extraordinary occasion.* Whatever that extraordinary occasion was is not known, however, the court was satisfied when a letter was produced in which Vice-Admiral Beaumont wrote that he desired Captain Hopson to do several things for him in Town.

The *Mortar Bomb*, a small vessel that carried 12 cannon, was eventually found ashore on the Dutch coast five days later. She was one of those ships that had been swept over the Goodwin Sands during the tempest.

As and when the destruction, that the storm had wreaked, was fully understood, the deeply religious British populace decided that this act of God should be 'celebrated' with a fast. On December 9th, 1703, a public proclamation called for:

> *Whereas by the late most terrible storms of wind, with which it pleased Almighty God to afflict the greatest part of our Kingdom on Friday and Saturday the 26th and 27th days of November last. Some of our ships of war and many ships of our loving subjects have been destroyed and lost at sea, and great numbers on board the same having perished; and great many houses and other buildings of our good subjects have been either wholly*

thrown down or demolished. Therefore out of our deep and pious sense of what we and all our people have suffered by the said dreadful winds and storms (which we most humbly acknowledge to be a token of Divine Pleasure, and that it was the infinite mercy of God that we and our people were not hereby wholly destroyed) are putting our trust in the Almighty God, that upon our humiliation and repentance, He will be gracious to us and our kingdoms and will yet vouchsafe a special blessing upon to us and our people in the just war wherein we are engaged. We declare and do strictly charge and command that on Wednesday being the 19th of January next that this fast shall be religiously kept and observed throughout our Kingdom

It is truly astonishing that the genteel citizens of the 1700s accepted this disaster as a retribution for the nation's sins – as opposed to the cry of global warming or the resignation of the weather forecaster, in this day and age.

The public fast would, in some way, alleviate the spiritual guilt of the nation, which the storm had imposed; however, it did not ease the suffering of the French prisoners awaiting repatriation. Because of the death and destruction to the Royal Navy it would only hinder their dispersal. It was thought that the prisoners of war would give intelligence of the sorry state that Queen Anne's ships were in – which, under those circumstances, would lead to a renewed and successful French attack. This contemplation delayed their freedom, and increased their misery in the cramped quarters of the vessels waiting to sail to Guernsey for their exchange.

Another threat was realised by the Admiralty when they issued orders to Vice Admiral John Leake that: *… and whereas tis likely that the enemy upon their getting notice of these disasters will set forth their privateers from Dunkirk and Ostende, with design to spoil and plunder such ships and vessels as are in distress. You are therefore herby required and directed to use your best endeavours to put into the best position that may be, and to cruise to and fro about the North Sands Head and on the back of the South Sands.*

However, fortunately for the British, the French did not take advantage of the situation.

THE STORM:

OR, A COLLECTION

Of the most Remarkable

CASUALTIES

AND

DISASTERS

Which happen'd in the Late

Dreadful TEMPEST,

BOTH BY

SEA and LAND.

The Lord hath his way in the Whirlwind, and in the Storm, and the Clouds are the dust of his Feet. Nah. I. 3.

LONDON:

Printed for *G. Sawbridge* in *Little Britain*, and Sold by *J. Nutt* near *Stationers-Hall*. M DCC IV.

Daniel Defoe's book

DEFOE'S DEFAMATION OF DEAL

By the year of 1699, King William III had granted Deal a Charter of Incorporation that had severed the unwanted ties, and expenses, from the silted-up Port of Sandwich. In 1703, Deal was becoming a flourishing town. With the fleets of warships and merchant vessels anchored a mere mile from the new town's foreshore, trade would have been brisk in victuals and slops. Tradesmen and shipwrights would have been in demand, earning a lucrative living. Most of this new found wealth relied upon the local longshoremen to ferry the necessary stores, equipment and passengers out to the waiting ships.

Although the many taverns were busy with seafarers and towns people alike, the mayor of Deal, Thomas Powell, did his best to keep order and normality. He tried to enforce Queen Anne's Proclamation to suppress vice and immorality; and it was the whores in Deal that suffered the ignominy of banishment. The mayor also hung up his own proclamation for all to read:

> *Deal, 6th August, 1703.*
> *These are to give notice to all persons that keep public-houses, or that sell wines, ales, beer, brandy, or coffee, or any other liquors whatsoever, that they do not presume upon the Lord's day, commonly called Sunday, to suffer any person or persons to sit tippling in the said houses on the Lord's day. Also, to give notice to all shop-keepers, butchers, bakers, green-grocers, hucksters, barbers, shoemakers, tailors, and all other tradesmen whatever, and also all seafaring men who go off bumbing in boats, that they do not presume on the Lord's day to exercise any part of their trade by selling, or putting to sale, any of their goods on the Lord's day, upon their peril of being prosecuted to the utmost severity of the law.*
> *Thomas Powell, Mayor.*

Thomas Powell was a man of principles. These beliefs and religious devotion made him unpopular by some, however, he carried out his duties with exceeding enthusiasm.

In 1704 a volume was published with the title of *'The Storm: or, a collection of the most remarkable casualties and disasters which happen'd in the late dreadful tempest, both by land and sea'*, which would initiate displeasure and create a myth that was to last for three-hundred years.

It was produced from an anonymous author who collated eyewitness accounts, but also added his own comments regarding the great storm of the 26th / 27th November 1703. Throughout the pages there are descriptions of the tempest's brief and destructive history that is charted on its course from Bristol to Norfolk. The observers' statements are sometimes a might exaggerated, but each declaration is signed, dated and the town of origin inserted. Readers were led to believe that this was a true account, and even in the book's preface a warning is made that:

> *Preaching of sermons is speaking to a few of mankind; printing of books is talking to the whole world.*

And:

> *If a sermon be ill grounded, if the preacher imposes upon us, he trespasses on a few; but if a book printed obtrudes a falsehood, if man tells a lie in print, he abuses mankind, and imposes upon the whole world, he causes our children to tell lies after us, and their children after them, to the end of the world.*

That book has been used over the years as a standard text by the many scholars who have studied the chronicle of the metrological phenomenon. It is only when it was found out that the author of the tome was none other than Daniel Defoe, that caution was applied.

Some parts of the book graphically describe the happenings in the Downs and ashore at Deal. Selected anonymous passages are scathing and hurtful to the boatmen and inhabitants of the town.

William Clark Russell, in his 1889 volume *'Betwixt the Forelands'* comes close to recognising Defoe's faults. Yet the story, for him, is too good not to be retold, however, he wrote that:

> *The imagination of the author of* 'Robinson Crusoe' *is visible in parts, but there can be no doubt that the narrative in main is accurate enough.*

Defoe struggled throughout his life to keep (unsuccessfully) out of debt. His marriage to Mary Tuffley brought in a dowry of £3,700, nevertheless, that did not allay his first bankruptcy in 1692 for £17,000 and imprisonment. To say that he married Mary purely for her money might be a bit harsh as the poor woman bore him eight children, six of whom survived.

No matter what Defoe put his mind to – be it keeping civet cats to make perfume or becoming a merchant dealing in hosiery – his run of bad luck always followed him. Even his brick and pantile works folded just before the storm, where after the price of roof tiles went from £2.10 shillings (£2.50p) per thousand to £10. Eventually Defoe would be principally remembered for his writing abilities with the novels of *'Robinson Crusoe'* and *'Moll Flanders'*.

In the year of 1705, certain people in Deal found some of the contents of Defoe's book *'The Storm'* offensive.

According to Steven Pritchard in his *'History of Deal'*, the town's Corporation ordered that a letter be sent to the publisher and bookseller in London, to ascertain the name of the author.

They described the defamatory libel as:

> ...*several scandalous and false reflections unjustly cast upon the inhabitants of Deal, with malicious intent to bring a disreputation* (sic) *upon the people thereof, and to create a misunderstanding between Her Majesty's subjects, which, if not timely confuted, may produce consequences detrimental to the town, and tend to a breach of the peace.*

It carries on by stating:

> ...*that the person who caused the publication therefore may be known in order to be brought to condign punishment for such his infamous libel, we have thought fit, therefore, to appoint our Town Clerk to proceed*

against him in a Court of Law.

The offending pages in *'The Storm'* are, in the original publication, from page 199 to the end of page 202. The beginning of the former page starts:

> *And here, I cannot omit that great notice has been taken of the townspeople of Deal, who are blamed and I doubt not with too much reason, for their great barbarity in neglecting to save the lives of abundance of poor wretches; who having hung upon the masts and rigging of the ships, or floated upon the broken pieces of wrecks, had gotten ashore upon the Goodwin Sands when the tide was out.*

It goes on to declare that some local boats approached the shipwrecked mariners but did not assist and *they* were purely there for plunder from the wrecks. The observer is then anxious to tell his readers of one person who was prepared to help, Thomas Powell. Town mayor and slop seller by profession, also a good Christian, who, according to the author, deserves to be remembered *'...for his charity and courage in a town with so little.'*

The disingenuous Defoe

Defoe continued the story by disclosing that, in the morning light after the storm, Thomas Powell spied the castaways *'walking too and fro'* upon the Goodwins. With urgency, Powell made a request to the Custom House officers for the use of their boats and men to save the lives of as many as they could. He was met with a rude refusal; and eventually requisitioned the custom's boats, along with several other local boats, by force. He provided them with crews made up of willing townsfolk who he had promised to pay five shillings per head for every man saved. Under those terms, they sped out to the shipwrecked sailors.

Of the one hundred and seventy sail, which Defoe professed to be in the Downs the night before, only seventy were still afloat. The mayor's crews of stout, honest fellows saved and brought ashore above two hundred men, whose lives (according to the author) a few minutes later would have been lost.

Powell now had the survivors to feed, clothe and billet until it could be decided what to do with them. His application to the Queen's agent (for sick and wounded seaman) for help came to no relief. He alone, had fed, lodged and those who had died from hypothermia and trauma, buried. Again he applied for financial help – and again he was refused. This is where page 202 of '*The Storm*' ends.

Along with the complaint to the publishers, it was requested that further communication be made to the Jurats and Corporation of Deal and the letter was signed by Thomas Horne, Mayor; Joshua Coppin, Tobias Bowles, Samuel Fasham, Thomas Brothers, William Conning, Thomas Warren, Thomas Powell, late Mayor; Benjamin Hulke and John Pye.

This fine body of men, some past, present and future mayors, knew that the story in the publication was fictitious; and as proof they would have had Thomas Warren's letters to the Admiralty and Navy Board that would exonerate the libel.

Since then, however, these letters have been locked away in the archives of the Public Record Office. Over the years many modern-day historians have embraced Defoe's version – perpetuating the libel when it appears in numerous books and articles written about the storm.

There is very little known about Thomas Warren, Navy Storekeeper at Deal and future mayor, nevertheless he was an educated person and excellent penman. His writings flowed over the paper with barely a mistake and never an ink blot. He used the modern use of the word 'the' and not the abbreviation of 'ye' and, apart from a few words, the manuscripts have been undemanding to decipher. It can be seen that Warren was relied upon for his accuracy in his correspondence; also his treaties were penned almost as the events had happened – not a year later, as were Defoe's.

The employment of store keeper was possibly a lowly name for Warren's occupation; as his position called for astute decisions, dealing with vast amounts of money and being the eyes and ears of the Admiralty at Deal. He was also held in high esteem by the town's people and Jurats and was elected mayor in 1705.

As store keeper his frustrations are noted in his letters when the storm of the 27th November, 1703, very quickly exhausted his insufficient resources of supplies. When this happened Thomas Warren would hardly have had time to sleep; as his writings and workload went into excess over and after the period of the tempest. He was sending and receiving instruction daily, to and from the Admiralty, and it is from this correspondence that the truth of what really did happen can be found.

He began his discourse on the morning of the disaster by informing the Admiralty of the miserable slaughter amongst shipping in the Downs. He writes that about two in the morning several guns were fired from ships in distress, but there being such a hurricane it was impossible to stand, let alone launch a boat from the shore. In his words:

> *... if it pleases God they hold the storm out, which is something abated; the sea so bad that I cannot send a boat off and that I desire you will please to order a vessel or two down to assist these ships with provisions of stores to enable them to proceed where they can be better fitted; and so soon as the weather will permit I will be more particular as to their wants and whether any of them want an anchor and cables, I having but one cable in store and that for a fourth rate which I thought fit to let you know.*

At daybreak there were only seventy ships left from the one hundred which were anchored in the Downs the night before. All of these vessels were seen to be in a sorry state, some without masts, and all of them torn to pieces by the storm. He also observed five hulks aground on the Goodwins; two of them large, and one which he identified to be a man-of-war by the number of men that could be seen upon her deck. Although the storm had slightly decreased it must be emphasized that Warren could not send a boat off in such conditions. Unlike Defoe's version:

> *Some boats are said to come very near them in quest of booty, and in search of plunder, and to carry off what they could get, but nobody concerned themselves for the lives of these miserable creatures.*

Significantly it is the following day that Warren went afloat to find out the needs of the crippled ships – and not as Defoe claimed on the 27th November. He also sent Deal boats to the only wreck that was left showing a waft. The shipwreck in question that was flying a distress signal was the *Stirling Castle* and, with the help of a Ramsgate boat, seventy men, not the 200 that Defoe claims, were recovered alive.

Again from the archives of the Public Record Office, there are no accounts in any of the captains' or officers' logs that there were rapacious local boatmen afloat at that time. Deal was a compassionate town, and it is recorded in 1702 there were four hundred infirm seamen being cared for. The hero of Defoe's piece, Thomas Powell, must have been highly embarrassed by the story of his alleged courage. As a deeply religious and pious man, the lies about him would have been too much to bear.

An experiment took place on December 8th 2000, to observe if it would be possible for the survivors on the Goodwin Sands to have been sighted at first light. This day had been coordinated as credibly as possible with the same in 1703 by using the Gregorian calendar, which increased the old date by eleven days. Sea conditions on the day of the experiment were rough, with a gale to a severe-gale from the south-west wind blowing to force 8 and 9. The first light of day was viewed at 7:20 a.m., and even at a height of thirty feet above sea level, the Goodwins could not be seen (even with the help of binoculars). Therefore, it is safe to say that no men were seen on the Sands and, if they had been present, with high tide around midday, the water would have been flowing and the men swept away before complete daylight. Even at any other time of day, under storm conditions, the surf would be of such a height that the dry banks of the Goodwin Sands would have been masked from those ashore.

To add more insult to Deal and her boatmen, Daniel Defoe yet again creates an additional libel with a ditty from another publication *'The Storm. An essay'*:

Those sons of plunder are below my pen
Because they are below the names of men:
Who from the shores presenting to their eyes
The fatal Goodwin, where the wreck of Navies lyes
A thousand dying sailors speaking to the skies.
From the sad shores they saw the wretches walk
By signals of distress they talk;
There with one tide of life they are vext
For all were sure to die the next.
The barbarous shores with men and boats abound-
The men more barbarous than the shores are found:
Off to the shattered ships they go,
And for the floating purchase row.
They spare no hazard, or no pain,
But 'tis to save the goods, and not the men
Within the sinking suppliant's reach appear
As if they'd mock their dying fear.
Then for some trifle all their hopes supplant
With cruelty would make a Turk relent.
If I had any Satire left to write,
Could I with suited spleen indite,
My verse should blast that fatal town,
And drowned sailors' widows pull it down:
No footsteps of it should appear-
And ships no more cast anchor there.
The barbarous hated name of Deal should die,
Or be a term of infamy-
And till that is done, the Town will stand
A just reproach to all the land.

Why did Defoe feel secure with these anonymous rants? Perhaps it was the anonymity, or that he had *some* friends in high places;

although one of them was certainly not Queen Anne. In July of 1703, he had been sent to Newgate prison on a similar diatribe (or satire) against Anglican intolerance.

Again the question must be asked why the disingenuous Defoe had such a dislike for Deal. It is thought that he must have had an altercation with Deal boatmen when he was embarking on another one of his schemes in shipping, throughout the early 1690s, and bore a grudge that he would eventually redress. It could be surmised that Daniel Defoe would have had some sleepless nights at the thought of the Deal Corporation's summons as he was already complying with seven years probation for slander.

It appears, for reasons unknown, that the summons was never to have been served on Defoe. When this present author discussed the motivation with London barrister David Allen Green, he acknowledged:

> ... from my perspective, the failure of Deal Corporation's legal summons does not go far in supporting any version of the events at issue. There are many reasons why a law suit does not get anywhere. One is indeed because the defendant has no money. Or that the terminology was incorrect. But another is that the party bringing the suit realised that, on the facts, it will not succeed. The Corporation may well have been reluctant to press the issue.

Nevertheless, because of Defoe, the truth has not been fully understood for over three-hundred years.

Hopefully there is enough evidence here to make his quote:

> ..... If man tells a lie in print, he abuses Mankind, and imposes upon the whole world, he causes our children to tell lies after us, and their children after them, to the end of the world.

Valid!

LOST AND FOUND

In and around the Goodwins, it was documented that in 1845 the Brake Sands had moved westwards 700 yards; within fifty years, the South Calliper had moved more than a mile to the north-east; and in 1885 the Bunt Head Shoal had completely disappeared. These changes were all dramatic enough to be recorded, however, subtle changes to the Goodwin Sands happen almost daily. A build up, or scouring of sediment, can occur over a tide or a gale of wind and hardly be noticed.

It was the loss of the Bunt Head, and then the gradual disappearance of more than seventy feet in depth of sand, that was eventually to expose the entombed *Stirling Castle*. Even in the early twentieth century it would have been possible to walk over the grave of the warship at low water.

When the sand started to move in volume, it was the fishermen who would be the first to notice and exploit the new ground that was uncovered. The contour lines on the Admiralty chart were slow to be replaced and only in the 'Notice to Mariners', issued by the Hydrographic Office, would the gradient changes be indicated. Therefore, even on the charts of the 1960s a large area around the Goodwin Knoll was still being displayed as shallow and in parts drying.

In the past, fishermen would mark the new ground and any snags of sea-bed obstructions that they found, by using their Decca navigational set and a chart plotter. Although these were hard earned secrets, and normally closely guarded, there was camaraderie between the trawler skippers – who were always swapping Decca numbers of fastenings with each other. A lost trawl was an expensive item of equipment to replace and losing one would put unnecessary strain on their winch and gear.

Tommy Brown, the skipper of the forty-five foot trawler *Shelandra*, had access to these numbers and was not only curious to know what the sea-bed obstructions were but was also interested in local historical shipwrecks.

Early in 1979, a small group of Ramsgate diving club members, lead by a local coal miner Paul Fletcher, approached 'Thanet Archaeological Unit' (now Thanet Archaeological Society) requesting help and advice in participating in marine archaeology. The Unit adopted the group who became members, and were introduced to a neighbour of the Society's Hon. Secretary and Treasurer, Mr. and Mrs. Fred Wall. The neighbour was Tom Brown, who explained that he would be willing to give up some of his week-ends and take the divers over a number of the fastenings that he and his colleagues had lost nets on.

Over the summer months, and after several interesting dives, skipper Brown put the group on a wreck five miles offshore that was to create quite a stir. On 23rd June 1979, Paul Fletcher wrote in his dive log that they left Ramsgate Harbour aboard the *Shelandra* at 7-15 in the morning. The weather was good; wind was slight and sea state calm. Apart from there being a spring tide, with high water at 11.26 a.m., conditions were near perfect.

The first two divers, Roy Kennett and John Chamberlain, entered the water at 9.30 a.m. After they surfaced thirty minutes later, two more divers, Keith Young and John Cazier, accompanied Paul on the next dive.

The underwater visibility was around fifteen feet, and after the last diver climbed back on board the *Shelandra* at 10.30 a.m. they compared notes. Paul Fletcher was later to record briefly in his dive log:

> *Found very large wooden wreck, about 20 large cannon and ball - 32 lb and 12 lb. Could not get a true size of wreck due to low vis and strong tide. Wreck 100 feet and 40 feet beam. 3 onion bottles brought out at the side of the drop chain* (attached to divers shot line) *and 4 pewter plates. Position of all 7 items noted either side of the chain left on the wreck after the dive. Onion bottles date about 1690. Pewter plates?*

Their second dive of the day on a 'copper nail' wreck in Sandwich Bay was less successful, and the only observation noted was that they had only two feet underwater visibility. They returned back to Ramsgate Harbour at four thirty that afternoon.

Roy Kennett afterwards wrote:

> *...we found the wreck in 70 ft of water. After the divers kitted up they went down the heavy rope which was dragged into the wreck, underwater visibility was 10 ft. It was noted it was large* (wreck) *with deck intact in most places, although at this point the divers did not know the significance of it. They picked up all loose pieces, apparently cow bones and large tin plates, on return to the surface the bits and pieces were examined more closely, they were old pewter plates, and human leg bones. Diving had to stop because the tide had turned, and the current had reduced visibility to nil.*

The shipwreck appeared to be emerging from a sand wave that was leaving a large part of her port side exposed. In over seventy feet of water, the hull of the wreck was protruding twenty feet from the sandy seabed. Although the vessel was almost half covered on its starboard side by the steeply shelving sand bank, the decks were littered with cannon, cannon balls, blocks and cordage. There was a very large anchor, eighteen feet long, with a ring so huge that the divers thought they could swim through it.

Slightly listing on its starboard side, the shipwreck was lying on the seabed almost completely upright with only the masts missing. Although the wrecks forecastle, quarterdeck and poop had degraded, it was thought that these could have been lying fragmented upon the deck. The only resemblance of a mast, the bowsprit, was lying along with the beakhead below the bow, which faced westward – towards the shoreline. All around the hulk there lay a vast amount of debris and cannon. Although on later reflection the divers considered these observations may have been doubtful in the murky underwater visibility.

Diving in the waters surrounding the Goodwins is only permitted when the tide is slack, which is after every six to seven hour duration. The slack water safe dive period normally lasts a mere thirty minutes, but up to over an hour can be squeezed in when the tides are neaps and weak. Close to the Goodwin Sands the underwater visibility varies from six inches to, at the very best, twenty feet. The diving season is a short one, normally from June until September and the weather unpredictable.

An artist's impression of the wreck as described by the divers © D. Perkins

The following week-end the group again dived the wreck site, and this time their quest was to try and identify the sunken vessel. In only six feet of visibility they groped around the deck, finding some small objects. Two sword handles, some brass navigation dividers and four more pewter plates. It was on their second dive of the day that they discovered the ship's bell.

After the two hundred-weight (101.8 kg) bell was lifted up on to the deck of the *Shelandra* they cleaned off the verdigris from the

The late Roy Kennett with the ship's bell

46

bronze. There was much disappointment felt, when it was discovered there was no name inscribed upon it. This was summed up by Roy Kennett when he later wrote:

> *...all our efforts were put into recovering the bell to try to name our mystery ship, the bell was located still intact. 18 inches in diameter with the wooden hanging block still connected and approximately 2 feet 6 inches high. After cleaning, nothing was found except the date 1701 and an English broad arrow.*

This date and broad arrow would be of great help in eventually identifying the shipwreck.

Enthused, the five divers set out once more aboard Tom Brown's boat on the 7th July. Sea conditions on the Saturday proved to be 'lumpy' with wind speed logged as south-west 4-5. This time Tom had some problems with locating and getting a shot line onto the wreck. Again diving conditions were hampered with only six feet of underwater visibility, and their task of getting the measurements of the shipwreck was furthermore hindered. However, amid the cannon lying on the wreck they noted that one was possibly made from bronze or brass.

The following day the weather became calmer, nevertheless, their frustrations continued when the rope, which was left on the wreck the day before, fouled the trawler's propeller. Once again, the divers were almost thwarted when they encountered only eighteen inches of visibility and the outcome of two days diving merely produced three clay pipes and three leather shoes.

It had been arranged for the subsequent Saturday's dive that the group would be accompanied by two professional underwater archeologists. Although this type of archeology was in its infancy in British waters, there was a small faction of academically trained divers with an interest. In poor conditions Paul showed them around the wreck and they tried unsuccessfully to complete some statistical measurements.

On 19th July, Paul Fletcher and fellow coal miner John Chamberlain accompanied Tom Brown in the *Shelandra,* and lifted the bronze cannon.

The cannon, which measured five feet six inches, was secured to the end of the winch wire. The task of hauling it aboard was made difficult as it was unfortunately welded to another seven-foot iron cannon by concretion. It was to be the only cannon of non-ferrous metal on the wreck, and after the half-ton weapon was cleaned up it was found to be a Dutch six-pounder. The inscription on the barrel of this fine piece read, after translation: 'Assuerus Koster made me Amsterdam 1642'. It was later found that Koster was a famous cannon founder from 1618 until 1650. A broad arrow from the English Board of Ordnance was also stamped on the weapon; it was thought that this must have been a prize from a Dutch ship or perhaps a gift when we were allies. The number 6269, which was marked onto the barrel, arose from an Admiralty survey of 1695-1702. It wasn't until 2003, researchers found that this number tallied with the one which was in the survey – and positively identified the gun as coming from the *Stirling Castles* quarter-deck armament.

The bronze cannon on display at Thanet Maritime Museum

With such a treasure trove of rare archeological artifacts, the shipwreck's position had to be kept secret among the small group of divers, Dave Perkins and Tommy Brown. The trawlers Decca navigator, that was used to find the wrecks position, was adverse to atmospheric weather conditions – and often the signal and numbers varied. Although ashore Dave Perkins was doing his best to get the site designated, it was proving difficult, as they had not properly identified the vessel with a name. What they did know, was that this was one of the four warships lost in the Great Storm of 1703 – though which one, was unclear.

The frustrations of not being able to keep a permanent buoy on the wreck were also causing delays – as was pandering to the meticulous archeologists' methods of survey. Paul Fletcher summed it up when he wrote in the dive log:

> *A very poor dive. All dive time lost showing visitors around the wreck. These people have come down to teach us!? After today we might be better doing our own thing. Another 2 hours lost trying to find the wreck, but we cannot mark same until we have an order on it.*

The following day Paul's patience was further stretched as he penned:

> *As Saturday's dive, learned nothing, told nothing. Two pieces of wood brought out. What a waste of a very good week-end.*

As they probed deeper into the sunken vessel, more artifacts were being found. Two of the ship's kettles or boilers were lifted. These were made from riveted sheets of copper, four feet wide by three feet deep and of a hundred and twenty gallons capacity. They had a lead pipe ending with a brass tap to control the flow at their base. Mounted on bricks and stone which formed a hearth, they were situated below the forecastle. It was believed that these were used for boiling and cooking the crew's food, but with those combinations of metals it would have eventually been very harmful to the consumers' health.

Keith Young inside the ship's kettle

Without the help of the archaeologists they measured the length and breadth of the ship, and with the aid of datum lines, started to map out the wreck and its artifacts. The measurement from the bow to the stern was 185 feet and the beam was 57 feet. This was puzzling, as the dimensions were larger than any third rate ship of that time.

Large numbers of artifacts were being uncovered and it was decided that the group would only lift material that could be preserved. The immersion in seawater over a long period of time chemically changes items, and once they are brought to the surface they start to deteriorate. Throughout that first year one hundred and seventy-two objects were recorded and conserved.

A rack of six brass barreled musketoons were recovered, with proofing stamps from the reigns of Charles II, James II and William III. These heavy weapons would have been loaded with a quantity of small lead balls and used not unlike a blunderbuss. They would have caused havoc when discharged into a crowded deck during a boarding manoeuvre. Other parts of muskets and pistols were found along with a selection of gilded officers' sword hilts, their blades long rusted away.

At the forward section of the gun deck, a crumbling sea chest was discovered filled with navigational equipment. Amongst the brass dividers a very rare wooden cross-staff emerged. This instrument provided one of the first ways of finding latitude in the early days of exploration. Because of the importance and fragility of this find it was rushed to the laboratories of the National Maritime Museum at Greenwich for expert preservation.

The Thanet Trust field archaeologist, Dave Perkins, gave a detailed description of the finds in his book The Great Storm Wrecks. In it he writes:

> *Sand-glasses were found in kit form and in an accumulation which strongly suggests a chest or packing case. The glass assemblages make up into five sizes of sand-glass. Wooden components consisting of disc shaped end caps pierced for four side bars, the whole assembled by a simple push fit. These kits were accompanied by pairs of bottles of an appropriate size. They would have*

been tied together at the neck with twine and sealed with wax. One large sand-glass was recovered complete and had a washer of brass foil so pierced as to control the flow of sand. The different size between glasses is explained by the fact the larger glasses were for watch keeping and the smaller for timing the run of the log.

Some small personal items of the crew were found, a shaving kit, toothbrush, leather shoes, a carved draught board and wooden eating utensils.

The macabre remains of the long dead seamen were also present. Bones lay about, many amongst the onion shaped wine bottles. These bottles would have belonged to the captain and officers – a preference to the drinking of possibly stale water and sour beer. The divers found a leather tunic with the owner's rib cage still inside. Even a gilt candlestick was retrieved with a skeletal finger still clutching it.

Whilst all the diving was going on, the Thanet Archaeological Unit was funding and equipping the diving project. They were also avidly researching the storm wrecks of 1703, as well as conserving and illustrating the finds. They accepted that the shipwreck was one of three third rate men-of-war that were sunk on that fateful morning in November. Those vessels being the *Stirling Castle, Restoration* and *Northumberland*.

All the finds were listed and registered with the Receiver of Wreck, which is a government body set up to protect owners of lost ships and cargoes; therefore, every object found from the sea must be surrendered to them.

To safeguard the wreck site from rogue divers, the Thanet Archeological Unit's application to the Department of Transport for a preservation order was being considered. The 'Protection of Wreck Act 1973' is in place to oversee historical and archeological wrecks which are of importance, and to protect them from interference; unauthorized divers could face a maximum fine of £5000. The designation order to protect this wreck was eventually granted in June 1980, with a fifty metre exclusion zone around it.

As the conservation of the artifacts proceeded, it was noticed that personal identification marks were appearing on some of the items.

The initials J J were being found on the brass hinges of what was once a purse, a lead plate and the pewter table-ware. The ship's muster rolls, which were viewed at the Public Record Office, showed that the Captain of the *Stirling Castle* was named as John Johnson. The odds against this name and the initials being a coincidence were too great.

It was understood that the *Stirling Castle,* although built in 1679, was rebuilt in 1699 and refitted in 1701. The bell had that date as proof. With the extra recorded length of the seventy-gun ship, that should only be 151 feet, it was thought that perhaps that was due to a poor reading of the tape (a very difficult job under water). Other thoughts were that it was hogging, and the collapsing of the timbers maybe accounted for the initial possible miscalculated length of 185 feet.

Eventually autumnal weather ended the 1979 dive season. Dave Perkins summed it up in his book The Great Storm Wrecks:

> *At the conclusion of the first season's work, the wreck had been thoroughly examined and the extent of damage noted. A selection of easily found artifacts had been lifted, hinting at the historically valuable material that might come to light with systematic investigations. It was now possible to plan safe access to the sealed decks and to attempt to answer some questions of marine architecture. Plans were made to exhibit the unique material from the wreck at both local and national level.*

The Unit's team, along with experts from marine archaeology and the National Maritime Museum, crammed in a total of forty-five days of diving. Amazingly, the whole venture was kept a close secret among thirteen people until the story was featured on 12th February, 1980 in 'The Guardian' newspaper.

The work ashore continued with the preservation and research. Bleak House, once the former home to the novelist Charles Dickens and situated high on the North Cliff at Broadstairs, agreed to display the finds. It was only later that they were moved to the Maritime Museum at Ramsgate Harbour.

Preparations were also being made by the divers for the

following year. They had a transponder or homing beacon, which the company Decca had given to them, installed on the roof of Bleak House. It would facilitate the finding of the wreck at all times.

As the winter weather lashed the coast, the spring of 1980 was a long time coming. When it did, it was heralded by a severe gale at Whitsun. Eventually the divers managed to get afloat and after a futile search, it was discovered that the sand wave had reclaimed much of the wreck. They were of the opinion that the bad weather had yet again shifted the Goodwins Sands.

Not to be too disillusioned the group checked out the other Decca numbers that Tommy Brown had on his chart. These unknown fastenings provided two more wrecks from the Great Storm, possibly the *Northumberland* and *Restoration*. The condition of those shipwrecks did not compare with the *Stirling Castle*. They were in a state of collapse and degradation, with artifacts strewn everywhere. The bell and kettles were recovered along with a quantity of onion bottles.

The Isle of Thanet Archeological Unit brought the wreck of the *Stirling Castle* from the Ministry of Defence in 1980. As a novel way of fundraising, they sold 64 shares in the *Stirling Castle* to the members and interested parties two years later.

Officers wine bottles — with an average content of 1½ pints (900ml)

The '32 Pounder' breaks the surface after nearly three-hundred years immersed beneath the sea.

RECENT SURVEYS

After a couple of exploratory dives in 1983 and 1987, it was seen that the *Stirling Castle* was starting to emerge from the sand wave once more. However, when the government survey licence was available for the protected wreck site, diver Bob Peacock applied and successfully obtained it in 1993. The conditions of the licence stated that only investigation could be carried out with a look but don't touch policy. Veteran diver Norman Temple had joined Bob and would provide video documentation of the site. Between them they formed an organization called *Seadive*.

When the shipwreck further emerged from the sand in the summer of 1998, they planned a major assessment of the wreck for the following year. Preparation for 'Operation Man of War' had to be thorough and detailed. An eleven page code of practice was drawn up; which covered diving qualifications, site conduct and safety protocol. Thanet District Council was involved as was the support of the Thanet Trust for Archaeology and the East Kent Maritime Trust. A team of thirty qualified divers from the Nautical Archaeology Society were invited, along with the Archaeology Diving Unit (ADU) headed by Martin Dean. He was one of the original underwater archaeologists who visited the wreck when it was first found in 1979. Also to arrive from America were six members, both male and female, of the Maritime and Historic Society (MAHS), these divers were lead by Bill Utley.

A month before the survey commenced, Bob Peacock and the team from *Seadive* cleared the old ship of trawl and gill nets that festooned the hulk. In addition they put down a centerline to serve as a reference in the poor underwater visibility. Two main mooring points on the bow and stern of the wreck were secured. These were for *Seadive's Tusker II* and the Deal charter boat *Morning Haze*; any additional vessels were to tie up alongside the moored craft. It was decided that the American MAHS group would be diving from the charter boat and were to concentrate their efforts on the stern of the war ship.

On the first day of the two week expedition in the summer of 1999, a press conference was called. Television, radio and national newspapers were involved and informed of the work ahead.

After each day's surveying, a debriefing was held at the Thanet diving club's headquarters, The Ice House. Each and every member of the team had a job to do, such as the filling of air cylinders, checking equipment and getting the marker tags together for the following days dive. The wreck was being re-charted via a master plan with additions being added after each days diving. Vast amounts of measurements were taken and each artifacts position was recorded.

The American divers' descent to the wreck was from a mooring cable that was attached to the charter boat and the stern of the *Stirling Castle*. The underwater scene that they saw was best described by Bill Utley when he wrote his article for the winter edition of the 'MAHS News':

> The stern anchor line was moored to a large cannon, itself protruding from the remains of a gunport. Forward of this cannon, the port side of the ship merged into the sand at amidships. Aft of the cannon were two more gunports, one completely intact. The cannon for each of these gunports lie just inside the gunports on the gundeck. About 10 feet past the after gunport, the hull breaks. The exterior hull planking of the stern has fallen away, but the rudder still stands attached to the sternpost. A portion of the bottom of the rudder is still buried in the sand. The open stern presented a unique opportunity to view the interior hull structure, and the MAHS team mapped an excellent hull profile on the port side at the break. Several feet of the hull were exposed along the after port side, clearly showing the turn of the bilge.
>
> Around the stern and port side were large and small upper hull timbers, many recently exposed and looking for the entire world like they had been newly made. Most of the timber is still hard, and shows remarkably little degradation given its age. Just off the stern, on the portside, is what appears to be a swivel gun. Amidships the sand still covers the wreck, although some artifacts are visible on the surface, including the remains of a box of muskets and numerous cannon.

Forward on the port side, more hull begins to show, along with the remains of some gunports. The stem is evident, and when first exposed in 1998, the strakes were still attached. However, over the winter, the strakes started to pull away from the stem. Much of the starboard portion of the wreck is still embedded in the sand bank, and to the best of anyone's knowledge has never been exposed. Lying off the wreck on the starboard side is a cannon still with the remains of its carriage. Various small artefacts dot the wreck, but none recovered as the license was only for survey.

With each day, the sand appeared to be draining away from the hull and exposing more and more fascinating artifacts. The British team of divers discovered a delicate wooden log reel and it was thought that this was possibly the only one of its kind that had survived from the Queen Anne period. A brass candlestick and a sieve like utensil was also lying exposed to the elements. As Bob Peacock's licence only allowed him and his team to survey, they were fearful for the vulnerability of these finds. Various telephone calls were made to the Department of Culture, Media and Sport (DCMS) and the ADU (Archaeological Diving Unit), and their advice was to sand bag the artefacts to protect them from dispersal.

After a week of good weather, it became unsettled. It began to blow hard and contrary to the forecasts the winds got stronger and the rest of the weeks diving had to be cancelled.

With the autumnal conditions setting in Bob Peacock was concerned about the conditions and safety of the loose items that were exposed on the deck of the wreck. Accordingly, he discussed the situation with Martin Dean of the ADU. The archaeologists preferred that the objects were sand bagged but agreed to Bob's argument that there would not be time before the short dive season came to an end. After swift consultation with the DCMS a temporary surface recovery licence was issued. By the end of September and what was to be the last dive of that year the artifacts were recovered. Regrettably the wooden log reel had already suffered from the weather and had to be lifted in pieces for conservation.

Throughout the 1999 season 250 hours of underwater surveying was completed. This produced an updated site plan of the *Stirling Castle* not only in sketch form but also reliable data laboriously taken with tape measurements. Norman Temple managed to compile a quality digital video of over 320 minutes, recording the exposed timbers and artifacts which were at risk of degradation and loss.

Project diver Bill Utley summed up 'Operation Man-of-War' when he wrote:

> *There is something magical that transcends simple archaeology when you dive on an intact wooden warship. It is only once in a lifetime experience because three hundred-year-old wooden warships are not supposed to be intact. Except for the divers working on the project, no living human beings can say they have ever stood on the deck of any Ship of the Line, let alone one of Pepys' Great Ships. To actually touch the upright hull, and swim through the gunports of the* Stirling Castle *is a privilege few will ever have accorded. It's a feeling that words cannot adequately describe.*

Beside the normal survey of the *Stirling Castle* in 2000, it was noted by the *Seadive* team who had been monitoring the site over the summer, that the sand which had been cradling the shipwreck, was fast receding. Sediment was also seen pouring through the gaps in her timbers and hull planks, as it filtered out of the hold. Also, part of the keel from the *Stirling Castle*

Bill Utley looking out of a gunport on the *Stirling Castle* © *Sandra Blake*

was being exposed so much that a diver, if he was foolhardy enough, could swim underneath.

On the crumbling gun deck, the team had witnessed that a large cannon had toppled upside down. With the dive season nearly at an end, it was feared that important archaeology would be lost or destroyed from the coming winter storms. Bob Peacock wrote in the Nautical Archaeology magazine:

> *After consulting several experts in gun carriages, we discovered that no intact sea gun carriages of this period existed, although many iron cannons do. A plan was formulated to raise the cannon and carriage. Diving companies were asked to tender for the raising of the carriage and cannon. DCMS were approached for funding, without success. The fast track lotteries were also approached via the East Kent Maritime Trust. However, their fast track is normally six to eight weeks and longer in the holiday period.*

This piece of ordnance weighed an estimated three and a half tons and was over twelve feet long. Although the barrel was heavily encrusted in concretion, it was suspected that it was a 32 pounder. The importance of this cannon became even more apparent after some consultation with Nicholas Hall, a weapons expert from the Royal Armoury. He said that the gun's wooden carriage was possibly the only one of its kind for that period which had survived, and if recovered it would be an important find.

The decision to lift the cannon had not been taken lightly, as preservation of iron and wood takes time and money – as would also the cost of the recovery. Bob Peacock, the *Stirling Castle's* wreck site licence holder, and Norman Temple his partner of the *Seadive* Organization decided, because of its importance, to fund the project themselves. They felt responsible to rescue part of Britain's heritage which would have otherwise been lost forever.

The vessel that they hired for the job was the *Margaret D* a large 80 foot ex French decommissioned trawler with a heavy steel gantry aft. On 11th September 2000, weather conditions were ideal with a light south-easterly wind and sunshine that made it hot and humid. *Margaret D's* skipper, John Bligh, was confident that the lift would go well and the recovery simple. Old carpets, mattresses and pallets were placed on to the afterdeck of his vessel, underneath the gantry. The plan was, after the lift, to rest the cannon on to these to cushion the weight and limit any damage.

During the previous three days, Bob Peacock, along with the *Seadive* team, had positioned a nylon strop around the cannon and made the gun ready to be shackled onto the winch wire of the trawler. This had not been an easy job as the fast approaching autumnal weather had made the underwater visibility poor.

The lift went according to plan, apart from a wire twist that Bob had to remedy underwater. Another problem was encountered when it was realised that the gun was heavier than the *Margaret D's* skipper had anticipated. With the cannon too large to be brought aboard the recovery vessel, it was made fast to her stern and towed back to Ramsgate.

Later that evening the cannon and carriage was lowered back into the water inside the inner harbour at Ramsgate. It would stay there until a lottery grant was obtained by the East Kent Maritime Trust for its conservation.

After this money was acquired, on Wednesday, 16 July, 2003 the large piece of ordnance was raised from the harbour mud and placed into a tank of fresh water. Soaking the gun and carriage would assist in the process of leaching out the salt.

Following almost a year of fresh water saturation, the gun and carriage were removed from the tank. Several days were spent on cleaning the barrel and separating it from its carriage. When this was achieved it was found that the piece was indeed a 32 pounder and had a weight stamped on the barrel of 49 hundredweight and 3 pounds (2495.9 kg). Under close scrutiny it was also discovered that the wooden carriage had suffered from wood worm when it had been aboard the *Stirling Castle*.

Richard Endsor, a 16th and 17th century warship expert, confirmed that this was a cannon of Prince Rupert's patent or a 'Rupertinoe'. The Prince's patent incorporated a method of tempering the steel of the gun barrel and machining it in a lathe to make it a piece of high quality. This created a cost of over double that of an ordinary gun; therefore, very few examples of this type of weapon are in existence.

The carriage and barrel were then replaced into two separate containers of fresh water to await conservation by the Mary Rose Conservation Trust and the Arc-Nucleat Facility. It would be on the 19th March, 2008, that the cannon's barrel was returned to be displayed in the museum. The wooden carriage had been sent to Grenoble, France, where it underwent a complicated process of replacing the water sodden timber with a solution of acetone solvent. After a time the solvent was then replaced with Styrene-Polyester resin and when the wood was fully saturated it was hardened by exposing it to gamma radiation.

The ultra-modern survey vessel *Xplorer*, which was hired by Wessex Archaeology in the Spring of 2005 and Skippered by Dave Burden. Using a Reson Multybeam Sonar vast areas of the Goodwins Sands and the protected wreck sites could be inspected.

An interesting part of the *Stirling Castle's* construction was found late in the dive season of 2002; which was to make ship historians re-think the verification of the earliest date that a vessel promoted a steering wheel. Originally it was considered that the ships' wheel did not come into use until 1710; and prior to then, the steering of the ship was operated by employment of the whipstaff attached to the rudder.

The divers had found a curious piece of timber just aft of the position that the ship's mizzen mast would have been. The wood was 1.3 metre in length and 180 cm wide with a couple of sheaves in it. After some discussion with shipbuilding historian Richard Endsor it was felt that this could be part of the steering mechanism. He stated that: '...*the piece is indeed the wooden supporting block with double angled sheaves which carried the steering ropes to the ships side.*'

Therefore, in all consequences, it was possible that the *Stirling Castle* was steered by a wheel – if correct, this would be one of the earliest examples of this type of ship innovation in existence.

Not all survey work needs to be carried out by divers. The site of the *Stirling Castle* has, over a number of years, been electronically appraised with the use of echo sounders, side scan sonar and recently by Reson Multibeam Sonar.

In the spring of 2005 a survey was undertaken by using Reson Multibeam Sonar, and with this equipment an accurate map of the wreck and surrounding seabed was charted. The depiction of the image was so fine that the ripples in the sand on the seabed could be defined.

However, modern technology should not detract from the many thousands of unpaid, underwater hours that the amateur archaeologists have completed. Without their input many of the historical shipwrecks would lay unrecorded and looted – depriving Britain knowledge of its great seafaring heritage.

Again their input is tantamount to learning about the present condition of these shipwrecks and their skill at diving under difficult local conditions unprecedented.

Prior to English Heritage taking over the protected wreck sites from the Department of Culture, Media and Sport, Labour Party Chairman Clive Soley (now Baron Soley) visited the *Stirling*

Castle. On Friday 21st July, 2000, he boarded *Seadive's* vessel *Tusker II* and his aim was to see first hand the conditions of this shipwreck.

On the way out to the wreck site he stated to the reporter that:

> *'What I'm interested in is to try and work out a system by which we can prioritise these underwater wrecks. After all, we can spend an awful lot of money on some of these wrecks. The Mary Rose, as I understand it, cost an enormous amount to raise and then conserve on shore. You are not going to be able to do that on every one. You are certainly not going to be able to afford to do it. So we need some ways of saying "Look, this is a particularly important wreck. We want to find out as much as we can before it is destroyed." And then you may want some special arrangements for particular wrecks of great importance.'*

Although his previous dive experience had been in the near-perfect surroundings of the Red Sea, 18 months before, he was determined to dive on that day.

On the wreck site, conditions were far from ideal. A north-east wind had made the sea lumpy and underwater visibility negligible. Norman Temple, co-ordinator of *Seadive* gave Mr. Soley the opportunity of cancelling the dive, nonetheless, the MP was determined – a decision that he would later regret. Tony Sutton, a diving reporter, recorded the experience in an internet blog 'Divernet News':

> *'Feeling your way down a shotline in tea-like water to explore an unfamiliar wreck while a nor'easter is playing merry hell on the surface is not a good idea, but to lose the line in such conditions is madness. I had no choice. I was thrust aside by one of that rare breed of divers, an MP. In a cloud of bubbles Clive Soley swept past. He was hauling himself up the line, hand over hand, arms shaking, face grim, fighting for the surface.*
> *I tried to follow but lost him. Visibility was about 15cm. I*

> *couldn't tell whether his buddy Nigel, a police inspector, was with him. When I reached the surface Soley was on his back, being tossed about by the waves like a rag doll. He had spat out his mouthpiece, the sea was breaking over his head and he was taking in water.*
>
> *Nigel was nearby, but perhaps didn't have a clear view. "Get his mouthpiece in and inflate his lifejacket," I shouted across. Dive boat* Tusker II *swung into action but in the heavy swell it took time to get Soley back on board. He was quiet as the boat punched its way back the six miles to Ramsgate Harbour.'*

The MP later said:

> *"I couldn't take the blackness. It wasn't what I was expecting."*

For Soley, this trip had been arranged to publicise the problems facing voluntary organizations such as *Seadive*. As reporter Tony Sutton explained the *Stirling Castle's* wreck site licensee, Bob Peacock's dilemma:

> *...he and other volunteers have spent a considerable amount of money surveying the site. He reckoned that it would cost £50,000 a season to do commercially what they do for free on the* Stirling Castle, *including cost of boat charter, diving and photographic equipment and paying a team of four divers plus a boatman.*

It was unrecorded what the MP's memories of that dive were? He was obviously enlightened to the conditions that these unpaid divers had to work in. However, that was the last that *Seadive* ever heard from Lord Soley!

Investigations from the 2007 dive season found the wreck in a state of almost degradation. Much of the exposed timbers had broken away and the sand encroaching over what was left. This sad sight was met with expectation and regret. Once again history is being repeated – and opportunities lost forever.

The demi-cannon's forward trucks were removed, along with the blocks, before it was lifted from the wreck of the *Stirling Castle*.

After three years immersion in Ramsgate Harbour the cannon is removed for further conservation.

THE MUSTER LIST

The *Stirling Castle's* muster list is an important manuscript, not only because it was the last document to have left the ill-fated ship, but also because it is an insight into the social history of Queen Anne's navy. Along with the ship's pay list, it recalls the movement and welfare of the men aboard. It was James Beverly, muster-master, who did the final check and brought it ashore on the 24th November, 1703.

For the crew, (according to what has been written) their lot was reasonable and fair. It was a vocation that many went into and took a pride in their calling. The opportunity to climb the ladder of promotion was based upon the sailor's ability as opposed to class. Obviously, the better educated - although many *could* read and write - would reach their goal quicker than others.

The introduction of 'Volunteers per Order' (only two allowed aboard a third rate at this period) were the sons of 'gentlemen', however, they had to learn the ropes over a period of three to four years of sea time; and only then, after a written examination, would be allowed to become officers.

A Swabber

The well-being of the men in the ships was paramount, as their skills were hard to come by. On board, if the seamen fell sick, they would be accommodated by the ship's surgeon. If the illness or wound needed longer to mend then they would be sent to the hospital ships that followed the fleet. When these vessels docked or anchored, the men would be transferred to the boarding houses or inns ashore. It would be up to the Admiralty to pay the landladies one shilling (5 pence) a day to care for their charges, until they were fit enough (hopefully) to re-join the service. There was also compensation or a pension for the loss of limb or disablement; this along with the hospitalisation would be paid (compulsory) by the seamen from their wages. This form of instalment, one shilling and six pennies (7½p) a month, was added into the pay list, and deducted from their earnings under the columns of *Chatham Chest* and *Greenwich Hospital*. It must be noted that part of this money also went towards the remuneration of the surgeon and the chaplain – for the sailors' onboard physical and spiritual welfare.

They were allocated a decent weekly food allowance of 7 lb biscuits, 4 lb beef, 2 lb pork, 2 pints of peas, some fish, 6 oz butter, 12 oz of cheese and 7 gallons of beer. If there was a shortage of food and drink, the crew would have a slight increase in their wage which would be noted over that period of time as 'short allowance'. This finance would have been worked out as a computation from the percentage of lack of victuals.

Unfortunately wages were difficult to come by and the seamen's wives always suffered; and most times it was up to them to find employment to get by until their husbands were paid. After the storm of 1703, it was from the monarch's compassion (known as Queen Anne's bounty) that the dead sailors' dependents received the wages that were due at the time of their loss. This imbursement would normally only have been paid in the event of the seamen being killed in battle.

Being on board ship for a long period of time, the men's personal needs were catered for by the purser. He would supply them with tobacco and clothing from the slops. Their garb would be hard wearing ordinary clothes as there was no standardised dress being used by the navy at that time – only the marines wore a uniform. Occasionally when a comrade died they would bid for his clothes. This was not so much as coveting a companion's fashion statement as opposed to a show of affection to the departed and his family, to whom the money would be paid. All of these financial declarations were logged and entered into the pay list under the headings of: *Slop-Cloaths, Dead Mens Cloaths* and *Tobacco*.

With a larger complement of men on board the man-of-war than a merchant vessel, their workload was not as heavy and they had a little more time to themselves between watches. Finding their own amusement would take the form of singing and dancing, accompanied by the instruments that they could play and keep on the ship. Games of dominos and draughts were also popular and the remnants of these were found by the divers on the wreck of the *Stirling Castle*.

Discipline aboard any ship had to be strict. If orders were not obeyed as soon as they were given it could not only jeopardise the vessel but also the crew. Floggings did happen, however, in Queen Anne's Navy the men were often fined an amount of two shillings and sixpence (12½p) for a misdemeanour. The *Stirling Castle's* swabber, William Gittings, seemed to be one of the biggest culprits on board as he massed up a total of fifteen shillings in charges. It must be remembered, his job of cleaning and fumigating the heads was not one to be envied. His misconduct was only surpassed by John Carrington, ordinary seaman, John Swain, carpenter's crew and Thomas Skinner, able bodied seaman, whom managed to amount seventeen shillings and six pennies respectively. In the pay book, these deductions were headed under the column *Neglect*. With an average wage of six shillings (30p) a week, possibly these fines did have a justifying affect on the men.

Being aboard a sailing warship of that time, their rank or *Quality* was somewhat different to today's modern navy. Although there were still the known titles of captain, lieutenants, master, midshipmen, boatswain, quartermaster and cook. All of these sailors would have their mates and servants under them. On the *Stirling Castle*, Captain Johnson had a total of fifteen servants. This did not mean that he had a life of luxury, as these young men were known as 'Captains service entry' and it was up to Johnson to teach them how to obtain a commissioned rank. Likewise for the other officers and petty officers, again they had a responsibility to train their servants and mates into aspiring candidates of themselves.

The ordinary seaman was a person of one year's sea time who evolved into the rank of able bodied seaman after a period of two years. Their employment on deck and in the rigging was one of many tasks – and in their numbers they were the core that kept the ship running smoothly.

Another rank, 'yeoman of the sheets' could be described as the sailing ship's 'engineer'. Without his expertise of making sure that the ropes, which controlled the sails and rigging, were in good order, then the ship could not operate. He would additionally work with the boatswain and sailmaker. Equally the 'yeoman of the powder' was also of importance on a man-of-war and he ensured the gun powder was dry and of the right texture. The armourer was accountable for maintaining the ordnance and had to answer to the gunner. Quarter gunners were responsible for the multiples of four cannons, nevertheless, on the *Stirling Castle* they were liable to tend a slightly higher number of guns.

A most necessary part of the crew's food and drink were stored in the barrels kept aboard the *Stirling Castle*. For any to leak, would establish a shortage of beer or water and hardship to the men. It would be up to the ship's cooper to maintain these, as his expertise with the staves and banding was above the carpenter's.

James Hawes was the ship's trumpeter. He would use his instrument to sound the notes of command that could sometimes be misunderstood or not heard in the heat of battle or a gale.

According to the *Stirling Castle's* muster register, from July 1st, 1702 until 27th November, 1703, a total of 590 names (455 seamen, 135 marines) were listed. Many of these men left the ship for various reasons. Two volunteers per order, one captain's servant and five ordinary seamen were lent to the *Monmouth* (*DFS* or Discharged From Ship) for a couple of days before being returned, and by doing so their names appear twice on the muster. Other ways of indicating the whereabouts of the men were penned in by using the heading letters demonstrating their destination. Leaving the ship because of being infirm or discharged (*DSQ* or Discharged to Sick Quarters and *D* or Discharged); leaving the ship dead (*DD* or Discharged Dead); deserting from the ship (R or Run).

In a breakdown of the numbers of movements of men on the *Stirling Castle* in 1702, are 53 seamen *DFS* or *DSQ* (some returned), 27 were *D*, 9 had *R*, and 4 had been *DD*. In 1703, 28 seamen were discharged from the ship or to sick quarters (some returned), 14 were discharged, 28 had deserted and 4 died. Of the 135 named marines, 21 were discharged from the ship, 4 were discharged, 15 had died and a total of 14 had deserted at various ports of call on the *Stirling Castle's* voyages.

The *Stirling Castle's* normal complement should have been 440 but was only 361 (officers and seamen 285) as she entered the Downs leaving her 79 short. The marines numbered 76. The crews complement for that voyage could not have been helped when a total of 36 sailors and marines ran (deserted) at Plymouth before she set sail with the Mediterranean flotilla.

Ten days before the storm, Captain Johnson 'lent' six men to a merchant ship. They were the master's mate Robert Drew, two captain's servants, Henry Doble and William Reed, able seaman Daniel Villure and two ordinary seaman, Cornelius Roberts and Daniel Stevens. It is difficult to say if they returned to the *Stirling Castle* before she was lost as the muster book had been removed from the ship on the 24th November. However, some of these men did survive to collect their pay.

Two infirm seamen and a sick marine left the ship in the Downs (with the body of a dead marine) on the 19th November, to be landed at Deal. Days later, on the 22 November, the remaining seventy-four marines were transferred to another ship. Colonel Saunderson's two companies of sea-soldiers were fortunate enough to be dispatched aboard the *Royal Oak* which weathered the storm; nevertheless, the men did not disembark on to dry land until her arrival at Chatham on the 11th December.

Although the *Stirling Castle's* first lieutenant, Benjamin Barnett, lost his life on the shipwreck, it is pleasing to know that this unfortunate incident did not deter his son's ambitions of a naval career. Curtis Barnett joined the Royal Navy, and as a captain, allegedly, found and captured the pirates John Rackham, Anne Bonny and Mary Reid. Rackham, better known as Calico Jack, was hung and then gibbeted at Deadman's Cay, Jamaica in 1720. Barnett eventually became commodore of the East Indies squadron.

Very little knowledge has been gained regarding Captain Johnson from his correspondence, now kept in the National Archives. From the communications that were viewed, it emerges that he was a competent and respected officer. At the time of the disaster there appears to have been a bundle of letters that were to be delivered to Johnson aboard the *Stirling Castle*, which for obvious reasons never reached him. The contents of these are unknown – sadly, perhaps they were from his family – however, the Admiralties representative in Deal, Thomas Warren, wrote, two days after the storm:

I do herewith return you (Admiralty) *a packet that came for Captain Johnson of the* Stirling Castle, *which could not be delivered before she was lost, by reason of bad weather.*

On January 20th, 1704, Johnson's daughter Mary, collected his pay of £347-2s-6d plus 19s 6d short allowance money on his victuals. His daughter also had the employment of administering the Admiralty payments to all of the dependents of the captain's servants, for whom her father was responsible.

To be plac'd Folio 222

A LIST *of such of Her Majesty's Ships, with their Commanders Names, as were cast away by the* Violent Storm *on* Friday Night *the* 26th *of* November 1703. *the Wind having been from the* S.W. *to* W.S.W. *and the Storm continuing from about Midnight to past Six in the Morning.*

Rates.	Ships.	Number of Men before the Storm.	Guns	Commanders.	Places where Loft.	
Fourth	Reserve	258	54	John Anderson	Yarmouth Roads	Her Captain, Purser, Master, Chyrurgeon, Clerk and Sixteen Men were Ashoar, the rest drowned.
Third	Northumberland	253	70	James Greenway		All their Men lost.
	Restoration	386	70	Fleetwood Emes		
	Sterling Castle	349	70	John Johnson	Goodwin Sands	Third Lieutenant, Chaplain, Cook Chyrurgeon's Mate; four Marine Captains, and sixty-two Men saved.
Fourth	Mary	273	64	Rear Admiral Beaumont, Edward Hopson		Only one Man saved by Swimming from Wreck to Wreck, and getting to the Sterling Castle; the Captain Ashoar, as also the Purser.
	Vigo	212	54	Thomas Long	Holland	Her Company saved except four.
Bomb-Vessel	Mortar	59	12	Baymond Raymond		
Advice Boat	Eagle	42	40	Nathan. Bostock	Selsey	Their Officers and Men saved
Third	Resolution	221	70	Thomas Liell	Pemsey	
Fourth	Newcastle	233	46	William Carter	Drove from Spithead, and lost upon the Coast near Chichester.	Carpenter and twenty-three Men saved.
Storeship	Canterbury	32	8	Thomas Blake	Bristol	Captain and twenty-five Men drown'd; the Ship recover'd, and order'd to be sold.
Bomb-Vessel	Portsmouth	44	4	George Hawes	Nore	Officers and Men lost.

The Van Guard, a Second Rate, was over-set at Chatham, but no Men lost, the Ship not being fitted out.

A page from Defoe's book 'The Storm' giving explicit details of navy losses.

71

The officers and crew who were aboard the *Stirling Castle* on the night that she was lost: (Those who were rescued from the wreck on 28.11.1703 have (S) alongside their name)

Captain/Commander:	John Johnson	
Captains servants:	Andrew Hobbs	John Jennings
	Robert Drew	Richard Young
	John Pedan	Peter Mothom
	George George	William Collings
	Robert Stevens	Nichola Campins
	Thomas Hymers	John Haywood
	Henry Wright	
Captain's Clerk:	Richard Benford	
1st Lieutenant:	Benjamin Barnett	
1st Lieutenant's Servant:	William Jones	
2nd Lieutenant:	Thomas Parsons	
2nd Lieutenant's Servant:	Samuel Hutch	
3rd Lieutenant:	Nathaniel Belsham (S)	
3rd Lieutenant's Servant:	William Goostree	
Volunteers per order:	Henry Johnson	Thomas Knyrett
Chaplain:	Thomas Harris (S)	
Chaplain's Servant:	Thomas Dixon	
Surgeon:	William Deas	
Surgeon's Servant:	Edward Moffet	
Surgeon's Mate:	William Christie (S)	
Master:	Patrick Bliss	
Master's Servant:	Thomas Owen	

Master's Mate:	Edward Driver	
Carpenters:	William Pellett	
Carpenter's Servant:	Samuel Hurst	
Carpenter's Mate:	David Davis (S)	
Carpenter's Crew:	Thomas Hariot	John Swaine
	John Pennybridge	
Master at arms:	John Green	
Boatswain:	Robert Partridge	
Boatswain's Mate:	Francis Combes	William Swinney
Boatswain's Servant:	Samuel Steer	
Sailmaker:	Thomas Durand	
Yeoman of sheets:	Robert Welch (S)	John Williams
Midshipmen:	James Robinson	George Emerson
	Humphrey Thompson	George Goodman
	True Hart	William Byinton
	John Ellworthy	Joseph Hamond (S)
	Robert Milman	Thomas Abraham
	Humphrey Bedlmer (S)	John Hocker
Purser:	Robert Hollows (S)	
Purser's Servant:	Thomas Green	
Cooper:	William Scory	
Quarter Masters:	James Candey	Adam Bass
	Henry Brimblecono (S)	George Pike (S)
	Thomas Clogg	
Quarter Masters Mates:	John Alexander	William Hart
	Patrick Reay (S)	Benjamin Smith

Cook:	George Howell (S)	
Cook's Servant:	John Holston	
Cook's Mate:	David Biren	
Steward:	William Hollocos	
Steward's Mate:	Lancelot Meadcalf	
Trumpeter:	James Hawes	
Gunner:	John Lawes	
Gunner's Servant:	Robert Jefferson (S)	
	Thomas Painter	
Gunner's Mate:	Richard Young	
Armourer:	James Norter (S)	
Quarter Gunners:	Thomas Willson	William Ibbs (S)
	Thomas Bayley	John Clarvise
	Thomas Jennings	Jonas Ryerson
	Robert Harris (S)	Abraham Phipps
Yeoman of the powder:	Thomas Smith	Richard Terry
Able seamen:	George Beaumont	John Beale (S)
	James Wood	Richard Edger
	Anthony Webster	John Smith (S)
	Abraham Chovin	Daniel Palfree
	Nathaniel Pantony	John George (S)
	James Carter (S)	Phillip Williams
	Henry Whitehead	David Miller
	Hamond Andros	John Worden
	Robert Thompson	Thomas Jefferson
	William Wood	Martin Cook
	Josiah Allyard (S)	William Willson
	William Curuthus	Thomas Cooper
	Stephen Cushman	John Castles (S)
	William Hutchinson (S)	Thomas Laverock

	Hopewell Green (S)	William Brown
	Thomas Skinner (S)	John Carbwath
	Charles Parting	Thomas Dixon
	Peter Skinner	James Keir
	John Curry	Richard Dell (S)
	Thomas Brown	John Barker
	Andrew Hannak	John Hughes
	John Lee (S)	Clement Revill
	Henry Hickman (S)	John Royson
	William Dymcut (S)	Robert Mackee
	Edward McCollum (S)	John Burnett (S)
	Thomas Osmond	John Knight (S)
	Thomas Harris (S)	Thomas Grubb
	Stephen Taff (S)	John Cole
	Richard Miller (S)	George Jacobs
	Francis Roggers	William Potter
	Zachariah Field (S)	Benjamin Penn
	George Duncan	John Tomes
	Thomas Blake	James Norton
	Peter Willson (S)	David Boyd (S)
	Richard Prichard (S)	John Harris
	William Rolph	Isaac Bussey
	William Wells (S)	William Hudson
	William Hustwait	Isaac Hall
	James Moore	Thomas Churchill
	William Dawson	Jeffrey Moncher
	John Paine	Micheal Hussey
	Charles Walker (S)	
Ordinary Seaman:	James Robinson	William Post
	Martin Smith (S)	Thomas Alders
	Joseph Hardey	John Black
	William Hawkins (S)	Daniel Leary
	John Harison (S)	Steven Hannor
	Paul Dobie (S)	Paul Eliott
	Alexander Fenley	John Hughes (S)
	Thomas Richardson	James Hamond
	James Ashbey	William Knight

William Watkins	James Smith (S)
Timothy McDonold	James Evans
Thomas Thrope (S)	Francis Smith
Alexander Clark (S)	Joseph Smith
Thomas Padwell (S)	Daniel Willis
John Carrington	John Edwards
Edward Newton (S)	William Ellis
Edward Banks	Griff Wilkins
Joseph Ford	Nicholas Blake
Thomas Mansfeild	John Cook (S)
John Shaklock (S)	John Bright
William Phillipps	William Carey (S)
Alexander Hogg (S)	Peter Mitchell
Richard Hodge (S)	John Phillipps
William Champain	Joshua Moore (S)
Peter Saverin	Edward Price
Thomas Hawkswood (S)	Robert Hobbs
James Keir	Robert Edgcome
Nicholas Haugherdy (S)	Denis Caine
Timothy Falvoy	William Deakins
Thomas Best	Richard Craggs
William Lingwood	Hugh Maxwell
Solomon Telly	John Gardner (S)
Thomas Law	William Clark (S)
John Harding	Thomas Thrailes
Edward Court (S)	John Shaso
Thomas Morton	Richard Wilkins
John Amsdle	George Sefton
Jacob Laforce	Daniel Girandean
Humphrey Humphreys	John Clowes
James Husband	Edward Stone
John Hamilton (S)	

Swabber: William Gittings

Un-rated men or boys:
Peter Maddison	Aron Reed
Moses Silke	Joseph Brown
Peter King	Edward Archer

Edward Hancock
Joseph Harris
John Guttridge
Simon Mercey
John Simonds
William Reed
William Kenington
Phillip Masters

John Walter
Henry Smith
John Hunt
Thomas Salter
John Whitton
Richard Hawkins
John Stoakes (S)

Additional men who were saved from the wreck of the *Stirling Castle*:

Seaman from the Mary*:*   Thomas Atkins

Marine officers: Winwood Marsham   Nicholas Shorter
                       Samuel Herbert   James Saunders

Thomas Atkins was washed off the *Mary* as the ship broke up. He then managed to swim to the *Stirling Castle* and was rescued.

It is a possibility that the marine officers were onboard the ship solely to obtain a passage back to Portsmouth as they did not appear on the ship's muster.

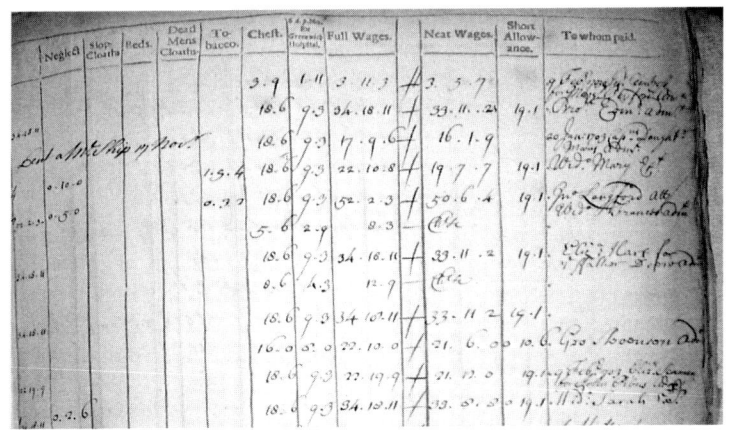

A record of the seamen's wages and deductions from the Pay Book   ©PRO

BIBLIOGRAPHY

'The Storm' (1704), Defoe, Daniel
'Great Storms' (1927), Carr-Laughton, L.G., Heddon, V.
'Historic Storms of the North Sea' (1991), Lamb, H.
'The Great Storm Wrecks' Perkins, D.R.J.
'A Captain in the Navy of Queen Anne' (1970), West, J.
'Betwixt the Forelands' (1889), Clark-Russell, W.
'Divernet News' (4.9.2000), Sutton, T.
'Shipwrecks at Ramsgate' (January 1982), Lapthorne, W, P.
'Stirling Castle's unique gun carriage' (April 2000), Peacock, R.
'Operation Man o' War' (February 2000), Peacock, R.
'Operation Man o War' (Winter 2000), Utley, B.
'History of the 30th Regiment' (1923), Bannatyne, N.
'The Command of the Ocean' (2004), Rodger, N. A. M.
'The Navy in the war of William III' (1953), Ehrman, J.
'History of Deal' (1864), Pritchard, S.
'The Greatest Storm' (2002), Brayne, M.
'Report from the Eagle' (1703), ADM/L/E.4. Lord Hamilton, A.
'Privy Council Registers' (1703), PC 2/79.
'Ships Pay List Stirling Castle' (1704), ADM 36/2606.
'Log of the Shrewsbury' (1703), ADM 51/833.
'Log of the Assistance' (1703), ADM 51/69.
'Log of the Eagle' (1703), ADM 51/291.
'Lords Letters, Orders and Instructions' (1703), ADM 2/31.
'Stirling Castle Pay Book' (1704), ADM 33/230.
'Thomas Warren's Deal Letter Book' (1703), ADM 106/3250.
'Court-martial of Captain Edward Hopson' (1704), ADM 1/526.

ACKNOWLEDGEMENTS

This book would not have been made possible without the help and patience of all those who have assisted me with their time and contributions — for that I am grateful.

Special thanks goes to: Robert Peacock, Richard Endsor, Allan Booth, Lieutenant Colonel E. J. Downham MBE, MA., Paul Fletcher, Dr David Perkins, Dr Peter Le Fevre, David Allen Green MA (Oxon)., Curtis Barnett. And a very special thanks to my wife Hazel.